Coming in Glory

Coming in Glory

Christ's Presence in the World Today

Martin Israel

Darton, Longman and Todd
London

First published in 1986 by
Darton, Longman and Todd Ltd
89 Lillie Road, London SW6 1UD

© 1986 Martin Israel

ISBN 0 232 51655 3

British Library Cataloguing in Publication Data

Israel, Martin
   Coming in glory: Christ's presence in the
   world today.
   1. Second Advent
   I. Title
   232′.6   BT886

ISBN 0–232–51655–3

Phototypeset by Input Typesetting Ltd, London SW19 8DR
Printed and bound by Anchor Brendon Ltd,
Tiptree, Essex

Contents

Acknowledgement

Scriptural quotations are taken from the New English Bible, second edition © 1970 by permission of Oxford and Cambridge University Presses.

Prologue

The theme of this book is the advent of Christ, the Word of God, in the universe.

He was in the beginning the one through whom order was created out of chaos, seen in our world supremely as the foundation of an ordered human society.

He is incarnate in the souls of all rational creatures, finding his summation in the person of Jesus of Nazareth. In him the Word was perfectly made flesh as he dwelt with the creatures of this world and died among them, sharing their agony. Through his eternal self-giving he raised the consciousness of the creature to a grasp of reality that transcended the self, embracing the world, and eventually identifying the risen self with the entire created order.

He is with us fully when we are fully human; the task of humanity is the lifting up of all creation to a knowledge of God, the raising up of the dead to new life.

When we are ready, when we have given up ourselves fully to God's service and have sacrificed ourselves for the good of all, a new life will come to us also, and we will see him as he really is. And so the Word at the beginning shows himself as the Word made flesh. When that Word is deeply incarnate in all humanity, we will be changed and see him as he is, the Word triumphant.

Christ has died:
Christ is risen:
Christ will come again.

The inner revelation that sparked off this book came after a severe illness that occurred about six months before I commenced writing. In the early period of convalescence,

vii

which was complicated by a severe bout of depression, I felt completely cut off from the usual source of my creativity. Prayer, which is usually the staple of my life, could then be carried out only by rote, for I was encompassed in a darkness that resembled a pea-soup type of fog. At the same time I was excessively sensitive emotionally, and past memories came flooding into my mind: I was overwhelmed by mental pain almost too acute to bear. But I continued praying for others, though no one needed prayer more than I. Suddenly one morning I was aware of a blue light in my spiritual horizon, such as is customary when I normally pray and am involved in the ministry of healing. This was my first indication that I had turned the corner of my depression, and was now able to see something of the spiritual realm once more.

Soon after this crucial experience of God's light I had an inner vision of the redemptive work of Christ in the individual soul. I was shown that the darkness symbolized a radical purgation of the inner life of all that was egoistical, so that, freed of all mundane dross, the soul could now be the repository of the light of God, to which St John likens the advent of Christ in the world. I realized how imperfect had been the list of my priorities in the past, how I had concerned myself about such ephemeral matters as status and income when my life should have been dedicated entirely to God and my fellow creatures, how providential had been my severe illness. I had been saved by my continued practice of prayer when all seemed futile. Then Christ had in truth been born in my soul, and a new conception of his incarnation in the entire cosmos had been vouchsafed me.

I had started this book with the idea of the second coming as its essential theme. Now at last I realized that Christ has been coming since the start of creation, and his final appearance is as much contingent on our ability to receive him as on the inscrutable will of God.

Then the wolf shall live with the sheep,
  and the leopard lie down with the kid;
  the calf and the young lion shall grow up together,
  and a little child shall lead them;
  the cow and the bear shall be friends,
  and their young shall lie down together.

The lion shall eat straw like cattle;
    the infant shall play over the hole of the cobra,
    and the young child dance over the viper's nest.
They shall not hurt or destroy in all my holy mountain;
    for as the waters fill the sea,
    so shall the land be filled with the knowledge of the Lord.
                             (Isaiah 11:6–9)

A Dream

I had taken a railway journey to its terminus, where I alighted. I had to ascend a rather steep, sandy hillock which I climbed without difficulty. After surmounting it I descended and soon entered a small seaside town that had an especially blessed atmosphere. The sun was blazing on the water and over the houses. All was peace and joy, and the people were radiantly happy. Their complete openness to each other and to me was wonderful. Then there appeared three priestlike figures with cowls, reminiscent of monks. They blessed me.

At once I realized I was among the deceased, and I said the blessing: 'May the souls of the departed through the mercy of God rest in peace.' Glorious as I found the atmosphere, I knew I had to return to complete my work in this world, and could not spend any more time in this heavenly place. I then awoke in a state of calm benediction.

1

In the Beginning

'When all things began, the Word already was. The Word dwelt with God, and what God was, the Word was. The Word, then, was with God at the beginning, and through him all things came to be; no single thing was created without him. All that came to be was alive with his life, and that life was the light of men. The light shines on in the dark, and the darkness has never mastered it.' So begins the incomparably majestic Prologue to the Fourth Gospel. Indeed, at the beginning of the creation story in the Book of Genesis, when God created heaven and earth, when darkness covered the face of the abyss and God's Spirit hovered over the chaos, God said 'Let there be light'. The Word effected the primary creative act by the power of his Spirit. The light was the primary effulgence that heralded the creation of the cosmos out of the chaos. The uncreated light of God working through the Word contributes its essence to the creative act by which material light was then to illumine the universe as it differentiated into form, life and will.

The Word was the wisdom of God, which not only made the cosmos but was also bestowed on it so that God gave of himself unsparingly for the creation, growth and development of the world. While the Spirit gave life, the Word endowed that life with purpose, so that it could attain self-awareness, ultimately to choose to know the Creator by an act of unclouded will. The primary energy of God was love: he gave of himself unsparingly so that the void might become populated with creatures that could respond to that love and grow in awareness as they participated with joy in the act of creation. God's free self-giving was not undertaken so that he might experience self-awareness, since supreme awareness is the primary quality of the Deity; without awareness there can be no love. But until that awareness filled the cosmos, God's uncreated light could never fulfil its work of creation which finds its end in the illumination of all forms to attain integration and manifestation as beings in their own right. Love does not seek its own advantage; its joy is to share its essence with all who will receive it, and its end in the raising up of all that exists, so that all that is aware may partake of that love and enter the full experience of the Word.

The Word is so close to God, bound by love to the Creator, that it is compared with a Son to his Father. By the Word God's creative power is made known, available and accessible to all who will receive him, so that they may ultimately identify the Father by the Word. What the Word shows in the world is the nature of God in eternity, or, as we read in the Fourth Gospel, anyone who has seen the Son has seen the Father (John 14:9). The Word, though beyond finite form, is intimately involved in the world; he illuminates the reason of all living creatures that are capable of coherent thought and independent action. The purpose of the act of creation is that each creature capable of response may know God, approach him in joyous anticipation, and participate in the life of abundance that has no ending. In our small world it was the human who was created definitively in the divine image. He was given the supreme privilege of knowing God while in intimate communion with him, an experience common to the greatest mystics of all the religious traditions, and with this knowledge to grasp the divine will so as to assist God in the maintenance of the cosmic order. Creation and maintenance are part of the same activity; the work of creation will continue until the divine love has been fully sent out into the world, after which it will return to its Source, intensified by the rational creature, with all that its creative energies have effected.

When creation was accomplished, the love of God was evinced in the soul of each sentient creature by an inrush of

joy. Conscious life brings joy with it, the categorical acceptance of independent existence and the emergence of the creature into an environment that is infinite in its potentiality for
growth and understanding. Whatever is given love and is able
to respond to that love, accepting it freely and without reserve,
flows out in love to all around it, and manifests joy that brings
the promise of fulfilment to all it touches. Thus Job, who
complains so volubly about his afflictions, trivial as they are
in the face of the living cosmos, is asked by God in the
tremendous theophany that concludes the futile intellectual
debate that precedes it, 'Where were you when I laid the
earth's foundations? ... Who settled its dimensions? ...
Who stretched his measuring-line over it? On what do its
supporting pillars rest? Who set its corner-stone in place,
when the morning stars sang together and all the sons of God
shouted aloud?' (38:4–7). They sang with the joy of creation
and shouted praise to the supreme Creator. The Spirit gives
life, while the Word informs the creature of the nature,
meaning and end of that life. The Word, God's Son, is the
effulgence of the divine splendour, the very stamp of God's
being, and the sustainer of the entire universe (Hebrews 1:3).
God's supreme gift to all his creatures is the knowledge of
himself that he has implanted in them and among them. In
this way they come to understand their origin in God and
their end in union with him. This is indeed the supreme
knowledge, not simply rational, let alone manipulative, but
rather unitive in its thrust and transfiguring in its intensity.

But love is not merely unitive, it is also directive; it accepts
us for what we are in order to direct us to what we are to
become. Neither the acceptance of love in our present situation, nor openness to its onward impetus are spontaneous
responses of the soul, let alone unconditional acts of will. We
were all created in God's image, in so far as we have the
ability to respond to the divine invitation and the power to
follow the directive to fulfilment of life. But we are also unique
creatures; the essence of that uniqueness is the capacity to
follow our own inclination and choose what we believe is to
our own ultimate advantage. In the creation story, our two
primeval ancestors Adam and Eve choose the way of selfish
advancement so that they can usurp, and finally replace, the

3

divine prerogative with their own stamp of authority. At once the soul of these two human creatures sets itself up in competition with the divine source instead of in collaboration with it. In so doing they establish their own separate identity incontrovertibly in the face of a universe that assumes a neutral, and eventually hostile, disposition. But they sacrifice their intimate knowledge of God, who becomes merely one of a number of forces in an increasingly impersonal cosmos. This exclusion, willed and selfish as it is, from the divine source brings with it impermanence and death; life resides only in the power of the Holy Spirit who is progressively excluded from the environment of self-centred, grasping humans. As materialistic self-interest grows, so does the knowledge of the Word, the understanding of the overall purpose of existence, recede until it is completely over-shadowed and occluded by the impenetrable darkness of incomprehension and meaninglessness. Life now assumes the character of a series of apparently unrelated events that punctuate time until decay and death close the scene.

And yet could the Creator have been unaware of the sequence of this cosmic tragedy? Though its participants are traditionally portrayed in human form, it is more than probable that their precursors inhabited the intermediate psychic realms as members of the vast angelic hosts of eternity by whom the Spirit of God is brought down to the physical dimension. We read in Isaiah 45:6–7; 'I am the Lord, there is no other; I make the light, I create darkness, author alike of prosperity and trouble. I, the Lord, do all these things.' That there is one primary source of all things, whether good or evil, is an article of belief in all monotheistic religion; it is not so much that God creates evil out of nothing as that he allows its emergence as part of his magnanimity. This is indeed a curious word to use in connection with demonic, destructive forces, but without their impingement on the psyche of all evolving creatures, there can be no growth. God, in his love, has enabled his creatures to grow into such self-knowledge that they can choose their own style of life to the end that they may come back to him as responsible adults and not as thoughtless, fickle children. Only thus can they bring back to him in heightened intensity the love that he has expended on them, or, as the Parable of the Talents would put it, 'For the man who has will always be given more, till he has enough and to spare; and the man who has not will forfeit even what he has' (Matthew 25:29). God's greatest gift to us is his love; his greatest power implanted within us is the unimpeded action of the soul which is the free will. It could indeed be argued that, had our ancestors eschewed the selfish knowledge of good and evil and remained in unselfconscious union with God, they would have lived in an eternal paradise unaware of their privilege in much the same way as a loved infant takes the maternal breast for granted. It is only when he ceases to be dependent on his mother's constant attention and begins to live his own life, that the child learns that love bears its own responsibilities and requires a positive response.

Nevertheless, the law of separation from conscious union with God is death. All things of their own have a finite existence; only in union with the divine is eternity known. In this respect it is important to distinguish between eternity and immortality. Immortality describes an existence that knows no ending, as likely to be hellish as heavenly, whereas eternity is conscious union with God, a state that transcends time and brings with it a transformation of the creature so that it participates fully in the life of the Creator. When God consigned Adam and Eve to a finite span of life that ended in death, he once again showed his infinite compassion; for them to have continued in a state of separation from him for ever would have been a punishment beyond endurance. Death, on the other hand, at its very least brings with it oblivion, whereas there is always the abiding hope of growth and development in supramundane spheres beyond our rational comprehension. And so the light of God which is the life of men shines on in the darkness of human ignorance, and an inextinguishable spark illuminates the way of even the most intransigent creature. The lifegiving wisdom of the Word may be spurned amid the meretricious glitter of the attractions of the world, but a spark of divinity lies in the depth, or ground, of the soul. It does not consent to sin for its nature is divine, but it is like the lamentation heard in Ramah, and bitter weeping: Rachel weeping for her sons and refusing to be comforted because they are no more (Jeremiah 31:15–16). However, just as Rachel's children are eternally alive in the love of God even as she mourns for them, so the person who has submitted to sin and soiled his birthright with filth and loathing is still held in God's loving light by that very spark of divinity where the Word is imperishably printed.

In our small portion of the mighty cosmos it is a privilege to be born human, for we are thereby given the power to know God in conscious recognition, to work with him, and to penetrate the most intimate secrets of the creation. We can think the thoughts of God, but also have the power to use that knowledge selfishly for what we shortsightedly believe to be our own interests, or else we can give that knowledge to the world for its greater blessing. The first way leads us to death, a termination unforgettably indicated in the story of the Fall, whereas the second way shows us, as a glimpse, the resurrection of all forms in the eternal life of the Spirit. On a cosmic level we see the way of this truth in the words of St John's Gospel, 'God loved the world so much that he gave his only Son, that everyone who has faith in him may not die but have eternal life'(3:16). He goes on to observe that the Son came into the world not for its judgement but that it might be saved. It is this incarnation of the divine and its transformation of the cosmic order that is the subject of our meditation. In this respect the cosmos embraces the entire created universe, and the cosmic order includes all physical realms tangible to astronomical investigation as well as the intermediate psychic realms that are populated by the angelic hierarchy and the souls of the deceased. The cosmic Christ is the Word of God who is also his Son, who fashioned the universe when it was brought into existence out of the chaos of non-existence, and who stands even more supremely as its ruler since the event of the resurrection of the incarnate Christ of human history.

2

The Spark

Though, in an allegorical sense, the human was turned out of the primal paradise in which he shared, albeit without formed awareness, full fellowship with the Deity and an accepted place at the heavenly table, he never lost contact with his own divine origin. God in his infinite generosity had implanted a spark of himself in the highest and holiest part of the human personality, a part known traditionally as the spirit, which in turn directs the encompassing soul in the way of true virtue. The soul, individual and responsive in the human being, is the seat of moral discrimination and judgement. It is able to divine what is right and wrong in most situations by following the golden rule of all spiritual teaching: do to others as you would have them do to you. It is only by such psychic, or soul-inspired, sensitivity that we can effect deep communion with our fellow beings, and then the message of inspired goodwill that brings with it a conscious commitment to bring love into the world breaks forth into our lives and fills us with a joy that exceeds personal aggrandizement. And so the Word was deeply implanted in the soul at the point of the spirit as a seed is planted in fertile soil. Though humanity has been forced to travel a long distance, material as well as metaphorical, from its original abode, it has never lost contact with its source, even if it has from time to time consciously turned its back on it.

The spark of God, his Word which is enlivened by the Spirit and brings knowledge about the presence and nature of the Godhead, is not merely a static principle in the soul, testifying, usually fruitlessly, to a higher meaning of life than merely selfish, predatory diversion and amusement. It is also a source of growth, maturation and fulfilment, at least when such growth and development are allowed to proceed by the sluggish, recalcitrant lower depths of the personality. For if the spirit is the repository of the forces of uncreated light that proceed from the Father in unremitting magnanimity, there is also a seat in the personality for all that is selfish, unclean, immoral and destructive. The darkness which is the antithesis of the light of God is also its complement, for in the final analysis every living form and every emotional power has its origin in the one Father who is the Creator of all that is seen and unseen. The drama of conscious existence lies in the constant interplay within it of darkness and light, of shadow and substance, of reflection and reality. 'The light shines on in the dark, and the darkness has never mastered it' (John 1:5). It has also never allowed itself to be totally committed to the light, preferring a subterranean, lurking existence to full exposure where healing and transfiguration could follow. This is the perpetual conflict between good and evil, a conflict that is disregarded or rationalized away at our peril, for the very stake of existence depends on the resolution with which we confront it squarely and without equivocation.

The spark lies revealed whenever we choose, quite spontaneously, the way of self-renunciation on behalf of a fellow creature, that he may attain the freedom of self-actualization, that he may become what God intended him to be. It grows beyond its primal form as a seed to a young shoot and sapling as it takes over more assiduously the conscious life of the individual. And so the seed of the Word germinates into this present life, assuming the initiatory role of mentor into the deep secrets of eternity translated into the language of the current world where we find ourselves. In every generation there are those few who have grown beyond the attachment to possessions and the distorted views the world has of success and wealth to a vision of wholeness that includes all creatures while lifting them up to the source whom we call God. In these few, the seed has attained the stature of a tree, the veritable tree of life, and under its boughs the compatriots of the spiritual master will find shelter and nourishment. Their end is to participate in the full life of their teacher, and so transmit the message to those who are to come later, the generations of the future.

The understanding of reality assumes different forms in the sacred history of mankind. One strand proceeds along an all-embracing monism, in which every aspect of existence is seen to be a manifestation of the Divine. Another strand points to a naked dualism in which earthly elements are identified with evil and death, so that the object of the fulfilled life is to pass beyond the illusion of material existence and enter the time-less expanse of the spirit where the ultimate purpose is revealed. Whatever position we may personally favour, in the end we have to accept the world as it is, a collection of diverse elements and phenomena that are to be aligned into a coherent pattern and integrated into a fulfilled whole. We have to learn to work with the elements of creation in solici-tude and reverence so that the entire cosmos is included in our love, to the end that the fabric of the world may be transfigured in spiritual radiance. Our lives attain fulfilment as we accept the creation as a whole to the point of sacrificing our own freedom of action, even our mortal existence, for the future development of the world. As one surrenders one's life, so one is granted a vision of reality that is all-embracing and eternal. The spark of God that illuminates the soul within each one of us leaps out in joyous recognition as it encounters the divine presence in the meanest responsive creature: deep calls to deep in the roar of God's cataracts (Psalm 42:7). It is on this basis that an especially satisfactory account of spiritual evolution is to be found in the Bible. It deals with the common people living unpretentiously in humble surroundings, and through the ebb and flow of corporate existence leaves them in this quiet, productive milieu gradu-ally coming to terms with the enormous reality that tran-scends the day of light and darkness, encompassing the entire universe.

The Word that emanates from the spark deeply set in the soul is the voice of God that speaks with prophetic authority. It is present in us all, but is generally so overlaid with the dark-ness of unacknowledged sinfulness that it cannot be appreci-

ated, let alone make itself known as a magisterial presence. It
is the apex of the mountain of conscience, an incontrovertible
focus of inner judgement within each of us that is disregarded
at our peril. Only when it is acknowledged and accepted can
the great work of transmutation be started. As we read in the
first chapter of the Letter to the Hebrews, 'When in former
times God spoke to our forefathers, he spoke in fragmentary
and varied fashion through the prophets. But in this the final
age he has spoken to us in the Son whom he has made heir
to the whole universe, and through whom he created all
orders of existence'. As humanity grows in inner spiritual
receptivity and moral awareness, so the Word incarnates
more fully in the entire personality and is empowered to direct
the human organism to its final encounter with God, in whom
all things are transformed to attain their full potency.

The glory of the fully realized human lies in his conscious
self-giving to God at the moment in hand. When he has lost
himself in service to his fellow creatures, he has found his
true nature, his authentic self in God. At that point in time
he moves beyond the form of a circumscribed individual, and
attains as identity that embraces the total human consciousness. As we read in the Prologue to the Fourth Gospel, 'There
appeared a man named John, sent from God; he came as a
witness to testify to the light, that all might become believers
through him. He was not himself the light; he came to bear
witness to the light. The real light which enlightens every
man was even then coming into the world' (1:6–9). The real
light had, in fact, been performing his enlightening work from
the dawn of creation, so that the indomitable human spirit
could sweep aside all obstacles from its path in its onward
thrust towards the mastery and reclamation of the world.
And now the light was attaining full incarnation in one whose
soul and mind were so transparent that the divine energy
could show itself at the present instant of time and point
of space by effecting a transformation of the coarse psychic
atmosphere surrounding the life of this world. The victim of
this world's greed was reclaimed through him by the forces of
light. The end of this psychic transfiguration was a universal,
heightened compassion that embraced all human existence,
being no longer foreign to any sordid detail of mundane

degradation. The essence of this change is not an escape by the victims of the world from their immediate situation or the general demands of life around them. Instead, all people are endued with a heightened awareness that leads them to assume an overall responsibility. This finds its fulfilment in giving itself without reserve for the raising up of all creation to God.

This is the eternal significance of God's incarnation, described so movingly in the account of Jesus' ministry, passion and resurrection in the Fourth Gospel. The sacred history of mankind, rehearsed with unique emphasis in the Chinese, Indian and Hebrew dispensations, came to a focus of climactic fulfilment in the life of Jesus, who shared in his perfect humanity the full working of the Word in our world and the final working-out of that Word in history.

The spark that is in all humans became fully incarnate in Jesus, and the proof of that total spiritualization of the body was the effect his presence had on all those with whom he came in contact and were as ready to receive him as he was always open to accept others. 'He was in the world; but the world, though it owed its being to him, did not recognize him. He entered his own realm, and his own would not receive him. But to all who did receive him, to those who have yielded him their allegiance, he gave the right to become children of God' (John 1:10–12).The feature that sets Jesus apart from all the other great teachers of antiquity – whose spiritual message, on the surface, has much in common with that of Christ – is his radiant presence that transforms all it encounters. It does this by yielding itself of its love so that the other person is enriched beyond material measure. If the beginning of the created order manifests the self-giving of God the Father, the transformation of humanity into children of light is the fruit of the self-giving of the Son. He effects this transformation neither by exhortation nor by manipulation, still less by coercion. Indeed, he does not strive to effect anything, but rather gives of himself freely and without stint to all who will come to him. He does this because his nature is love, and the essential property of love is its ceaseless giving of itself in order that all who will respond to it may become fulfilled in their own integrity and be free to develop into something of the nature of Christ, to become authentic children of God. Love looks for no recompense; it has no eye to future reward, let alone justification for its action. Its action, on the contrary, transcends the temporal sequence and works in the atmosphere of eternal values.

Love is not simply a spontaneous giving of affection and warmth to those around the lover. It also encompasses a radical renunciation of the person of the lover even to the point of physical dissolution. St Paul was later to say of Jesus' ministry, 'For you know how generous our Lord Jesus Christ has been: he was rich, yet for your sake he became poor, so that through his poverty you might become rich' (2 Corinthians 8:9). Just as he was aware of the power leaving him as he was touched surreptitiously by the woman who had suffered from haemorrhages for twelve years, so his entire ministry was one of unceasing self-sacrifice on behalf of those who drained him with the selfish inconsideration of little children. They, however, seldom had any awareness of what they were receiving, let alone any thankfulness for the priceless gift of the presence of the Son of God among them. Love, in other words, has its intrinsic debt that is paid without demur by the lover. In due course, the beloved pays that fearful debt too, but not to the lover. Instead, he gives of the love he has received to those around him, as his own life moves beyond personal acquisitiveness and vain ostentation in selfless, devoted service to the grey world of suffering and incomprehension that forms the foundation of our living society. The nature of love is acceptance with unflagging service; its end is a raising of the whole created order from torpid stagnation to vibrant activity.

In the atmosphere of John's account of Jesus, who is the personification of the divine wisdom heralded in the literature of the Old Testament, the Word is perpetually available, giving of itself without price to all who will receive him. 'Wisdom has built her house, she has hewn her seven pillars; she has killed a beast and spiced her wine, and she has spread her table. She has sent out her maidens to proclaim from the highest part of the town, "Come in, you simpletons." She says also to the fool, "Come, dine with me and taste the wine that I have spiced. Cease to be silly, and you will live, you

will grow in understanding" ' (Proverbs 9:1–6). Jesus says of
his eternal nature, 'I am the bread of life. Whoever comes to
me shall never be hungry, and whoever believes in me shall
never be thirsty' (John 6:35), and again, 'If anyone is thirsty
let him come to me; whoever believes in me, let him drink'
(John 7:38). Thus he gives of himself in the miracle of the
feeding of the five thousand, as he does also in the turning of
the water into wine in the miracle at the marriage feast in
Cana-in-Galilee. This miracle has an even more significant
spiritual message: anyone encountering the living Word is
raised in awareness from the insipid watery consciousness of
mundane existence to the fiery self-affirmation of new wine,
an affirmation that finds its end in union with God. This is
indeed the spiritual journey of the soul – from matter to spirit,
in the course of which the material universe is affirmed, served
and raised up to spiritual potency.

The end of the Word's life on earth, indeed the very heart
of his incarnation, is submission to the forces of darkness.
Though without sin himself, so that there is no cloud of
impurity to come between his soul – indeed, his total personality – and God the Father, he voluntarily enters the scarcely
penetrable fog of psychic evil that encompasses the world,
and starts to clear it. He enters willingly the satanic realm
when, after his baptism, he is led by the Holy Spirit into the
world's illusion to be tempted by the forces of cosmic darkness. He is invited to show himself as one of them by using
his superlative spiritual gifts to his own advantage, even to
the extent of claiming a world dominion in which to assert
an overriding power. But the other property of love is respect
for those to whom it flows out in selfless service. It will not
take over another individual, even to the minimal extent of
guiding him in the way of enlightenment, until the soul of
the beloved is alert and willing. Each person is infinitely
valuable because each is a unique child of God; each person's
will is sacrosanct, since it cannot fulfil the work it has come
in to perform until it is in the service of a perfectly free
individual, whose soul responds vibrantly to the summons of
life. When things went well for Jesus in the course of his
ministry among his fellows, all the common people received
him with rapture. The professional religionists alone rejected

him, because they could not bear to sacrifice the veneer of piety that hid their inner baseness. The common people had no shield of rectitude to protect them against the knowledge of the darkness within them, and so they could respond to the Word by an inward leap of joy when they realized that they were accepted for what they were. To respond to love can be as painful an experience as bearing rejection. When we are rejected we feel that we are of no use, and there seems to be no future to envisage; when we are dearly loved, we face the terrible fact of our own unworthiness, and are only slowly enabled to identify ourselves with our baseness as surely as we are accustomed to bask in the glamour of our more attractive characteristics. Rejection strikes at our sense of self-esteem that is often confused with pride. Love exposes our pride which will in turn shrink from the light of that love, until the pride is shattered by a fall that exposes our impotence totally and without mitigation.

When we know we are nothing and experience love, we can at last begin to accept that love and grow as people in its radiant warmth. The love has to assimilate the darkness of the world around it, confronting the baseness of so much human nature, in order to accommodate the demonic element in life. Only by a complete accommodation, a radical acceptance without pretending that things are other than the truth, can the darkness be lifted up to the light. Then alone does its powerful negative charge become incorporated into the body of living beings, and its contribution to the growth of mankind become positive and powerful. The darkness that is healed by love has a peculiar contribution to make to our common good in that it can in turn approach the raging agony of life and bring it to the peace of acceptance. Only that which has known the powerful forces of destruction, submitted to them in abject faith, undergone disintegration, and then experienced regeneration can be a worthy companion to all who suffer and are in raging torment.

Thus the earthly life of the Word made flesh ends enveloped in the gloom of doubt and the astringency of failure. First the acrid psychic stench of naked evil and despair are encountered in the garden of Gethsemane, a meeting survived only by the power of rapt prayer to the One who is hidden behind the darkness. And then the ignominy of public disgrace with its attendant malice is embraced on the cross of Calvary. It is important to grasp how far Jesus was from understanding the full import of his ministry and passion during the last part of his agony on the cross. Not only did God the Father seem to have forsaken him, but the validity, let alone the success, of his mission was sorely in doubt as the forces of darkness hemmed him in to the point of suffocation. The spirit that had been given to Jesus at the time of his conception was now given back to his Father. But what had he done with that spirit during his life on earth? Judging by the events on Calvary the spirit had achieved little to its credit, and the life of Jesus was consummated in futility. An agnosticism, holy but terrible in its frankness, illuminates the terminal scene of his ministry. Only when he died was his full glory to be realized, first by the Roman soldiers who were greatly moved by his noble bearing and calm acceptance. Later, his resurrected body was to bring a new understanding of the destiny in store for the entire creation to all who would pay attention and listen to the word of God. But first he descended into the hell of those who had died in the darkness of total incomprehension, so that they too might be released from the burden of guilt to enter into a new life of acceptance and love. Thus the Lord of light has dominion over the darkness also.

The darkness that Adam and Eve had brought upon themselves as an inevitable part of their growth into self-knowledge when they had departed from the heavenly fellowship, a darkness gradually to be lifted by the work of the prophets and saints of antiquity, was now, in the great event of Jesus' resurrection, brought into the full light of another day so that it could be finally delivered from the realm of evil. The spark of divinity that lies eternally in the holiest part of the human soul was at last finally cleared of the usual surrounding miasma of sin and could shine as an inextinguishable beacon in the world. As Jesus' physical body was changed to spiritual light, so the whole created universe was given its first glimpse of a total resurrection of matter to spiritual essence. Matter, though holy inasmuch as God made it, is coarse, corruptible and evanescent. The spirit, emanating from God's Holy Spirit, is refined, incorruptible and eternal. The life, death and resurrection of Christ, by reconciling the entire cosmos to God, brought about the preconditions for a total resurrection of the world. But first there had to be a resurrection of human nature. This was effected in the life of Jesus by his healing power on all those who could accept him. But the transformation, though initiated by Christ, has to proceed according to its own momentum. This is the burden of individual incarnate life and the basis of the world's history.

3

The Eternal Presence and the Future Hope

When Christ walked among the people of his time, he divested them of the protection of illusion. In his presence they saw themselves in their true nature and from thenceforth they needed no external embellishment to add to their attractiveness or worth. We are acceptable because God made us; it is the love of God that ensures our future both in this world and the one we shall know when we die. There is, in fact, only one world and our relationship with it depends on our state of consciousness. When Christ was with the people of his time, his very presence heightened the awareness of all who were open to him. From the usual earthbound preoccupation with its undertones of selfish isolation, his contemporaries were raised to a world-embracing response that included all created things. When Adam and Eve fell, they sacrificed their unique knowledge of God for a limited, circumscribed, specialized understanding of the world around them. This world was one of finite forms that cast lengthening shadows over the landscape in front of it, so that the originally freely-ranging human awareness was gradually closed in and diminished. The fruit of selfish acquisitiveness gradually assumed the character of a shrinking prison.

Whatever we appropriate for ourselves, thereby excluding our fellows from participating in its enjoyment, becomes our own place of limitation, our prison, and eventually our grave. Whatever our heart is especially attached to so that it becomes a focus of coveting, becomes our point of dissolution. This is because every earthly attainment has its end, and once it has passed away like a phantom in a silent night all that remains is a dark void. It becomes the repository of vain memory, the object of pathos, but its substance cannot be brought back.

The self-giving of the Father brought into being the entire cosmos. What should have been an oasis of unobstructed, unending bliss, a fellowship of souls without barrier, became an enclosed world of personal striving that deteriorated into a place of rivalry and covetousness whose end was death. The menacing evil that underlies the first eleven chapters of the Book of Genesis, and the course of moral evolution traced in this account of human assertiveness devoid of commitment to God or service to the world, culminate in the account of the tower of Babel. This depicts human pride at its most insolent, and the end is strife and discord so that the people can no longer communicate effectively among themselves. In the end they are deprived of the united will necessary to carry out the great enterprise of building the tower. Instead they find themselves scattered over the face of the earth, where they can no longer converse effectively as the thread of the common language has been broken. This thread is love; in its presence alone can a universal language be born in which all sounds become intelligible to the soul.

This account of thwarted spiritual growth defines with great precision the fate of human aspirations when they are not fertilized by a higher wisdom that comes from God. This wisdom brings a concern for the entire creation with it, and ends in raising up all life to the realm of meaning and radiance. What starts with deep aspirations of service, if it is not centred in God by the power of the Holy Spirit, soon loses its way. It becomes fragmented and malaligned as the factions contained within it war against each other instead of working together for the common good. The sacred history of the Israelites as recorded in the Old Testament is an ongoing account of an incompletely aware people seeking in vain for a power that will direct and integrate them. The power is around them, but they are not able to work with it because they are not capable of losing themselves in its service. This power of God leads them into dramatic encounters with an intelligence that far outstrips the comprehension of the human mind, but although they can accept its majesty, they cannot let it work within them. The reason for this failure is the domination of personal assertiveness that lies at the core of human personality. Only when the assertive element is surrendered can the power of the Most High find its shelter within the soul; in the words of the Magnificat, 'the hungry he has satisfied with good things, the rich sent empty away'. Were the people able to have accommodated the humble power of God, love would have entered their hearts at the same time. As the loving community developed, so would the new dispensation have drawn closer.

The self-giving of the Son did bring those who accepted his authority closer together, for, as St Paul puts it, God was in Christ reconciling the world to himself (2 Corinthians 5:19). He did this great work of self-dedication in his assumption of human nature, in his experience of the depths of suffering and the stigma of humiliation no less than in the splendour of a charismatic presence. In his own life the agony and the glory of human existence were brought together and united in death. And in that death both agony and glory were resurrected to spiritual radiance so that all conditions of human life were embraced and none rejected. The miracles worked by the incarnate Lord were produced primarily neither to confirm Jesus' power nor even assuage human pain. Important as both these considerations are, they were nevertheless the effects of something far greater even than their sum. The essential revelation was the nearness of the Kingdom of God. Even the most unprepossessing sufferer was a child of God, and when he had accepted the full implications of healing, he underwent a subtle inner change that released him from all dependence on mortal things. He was now infused with the strength from on high. Once the Kingdom of God was present among mankind, there was an inner transformation that brought people closer to the Father. As St Paul was to write, 'When anyone is united to Christ, there is a new world; the old order has gone, and a new order has already begun' (2 Corinthians 5:17)

It is interesting to study the change in perspective that the life of Jesus wrought on his disciples. They were summoned from their earthly trades to follow him; their call was to be fishers of men, but first they had to be cleansed of all mundane dross and freed from materialistic illusion. How wonderful it must have been to claim membership in that exclusive, yet unobtrusive, fellowship, to be the constant companion of the lord of life from whom emanated in a pure fountain of radiance the Spirit of God! In his presence all the answers to life's problems seemed to be available, while failure was not so much as to be envisaged. They were a fellowship that was integrated by the power of God and focused around the personality of Jesus. How highly the ignorant disciples thought of themselves, what honours in the life of the world to come they imagined for themselves and openly coveted! They believed they had attained spiritual mastery. And then the centre of their hopes, the focus of their lives and the meaning of existence itself suddenly appeared to fail. Jesus was led into the hands of sinners who had him condemned to death. The sinners were men strong in traditional religious practice who could not bear the light of God's truth to illumine the darkness of their own souls. How often conventional religion is used as a ritual to divert our attention away from our own shortcomings! God in Christ came as the authoritative Word to cut away the inessential trappings of religion and lay the soul of the believer bare to the healing power of the Holy Spirit.

He came in his own apparent failure to strip the glamour of his presence, the aura of his manifest omnipotence and infallibility from the obstructed vision of his groping yet self-assured followers. They had ultimately to be guided, indeed united, by a power more durable and constant than his physical presence among them. Even more important, they had to learn the paradoxes of spiritual living, that failure is the glorious crown of worldly success, that pain lies at the heart of the healing ministry, that death puts an end to earthly life in order to set in motion a true resurrection of the personality. None of the spiritual truths is to be understood by the unaided intellect; each is approached and made intelligible by experience in which the lesser certainty is sacrificed in faith for the greater hope dimly displayed before us but beyond rational conception.

The end of the Son's self-giving was the birth into spiritual reality of the disciples. The pain of Christ as he confronted the unspeakable terror of psychical darkness was transformed into the pain of meaninglessness that assailed the bereft disciples, a meaninglessness that was transcribed into a terrible loneliness as their master departed from their midst. With the departure of Jesus went all their expansive hopes for the future. They became once more as little children – indeed they behaved as such when Jesus was among them, but they were clothed in the trappings of mature men, as we all are when we stamp our way confidently in the world's forum. But when their centre was ravaged, the grandeur of a fertile imagination collapsed inwards, and they saw for the first time that they were nothing. This is always a key experience in the spiritual life; for most people it comes at the time of death when all earthly appurtenances are being shed, and then it is too late, at least in terms of this life. But when we know we are nothing, we enter into the uncomplicated world of the young child once more and can accept the unconditional love of God, who too is best known as No-Thing, available to the poor in spirit while strangely inaccessible to the worldly wise. Thus the shattered disciples began to know the world of Adam and Eve before these two yielded to the temptation of self-assertiveness without reference to God. The disciples' agony was one of complete self-disclosure, but at the end of the trial, when all seemed to be consummated in futility, there came an experience of the resurrected Lord.

The resurrection is, in fact, the first part of Christ's coming in glory. He came not so much to show that he was still alive, that death had no dominion over him, as to assure his vacillating disciples that the bond of fellowship was not broken, that forgiveness lay at the heart of their relationship, that God's most immediate quality is love. He did not come to his persecutors in his resurrected form because they would not have been able to receive him; his appearance might have terrified them into submission, shocked them into belief, but his way was not one of force or coercion. He came to his own and at last they were able to receive him, at least to their limited capacity. When Christ rose from the dead he took his whole earthly personality with him; he showed us a completely resurrected person, but the physical body was

21

transformed into spiritual essence, since flesh and blood can never possess immortality (1 Corinthians 15:50). This resurrection of the body is our assurance that all aspects of mortal existence are in the providence of God, that nothing is too mean or insignificant for his attention, that everything is worthy of new life in the power of the divine love. This free offering of love lies at the heart of healing, but it requires the free will of the creature no less than the unreserved self-giving of the Creator. When the disciples, to their unutterable amazement and speechless joy, were confronted with the risen Christ, they had attained a knowledge of the Kingdom of God, for at last they had moved beyond the isolation of personal acquisitiveness to the sharing of individual bliss in a transformed community. In this way the world of Adam and Eve before the Fall, prepared-for during the period of dereliction before Christ showed himself again, was also made manifest: they had attained that experience of union by pure grace. Their behaviour would have appeared to merit their total rejection by their risen Lord, but instead he came to them as pure, embracing love. The spirit had been willing even though the flesh was weak. Now had come the time for the strengthening of the flesh also as a preparation for the resurrection of the body ahead of all of us. Furthermore, survival of death can be known in our life only through the power of love. He who loves can never be finally separated from the beloved, and to love requires one to know oneself in truth, for one's love is a reflection of the divine love that illuminates all on which its rays impinge. Our existence is a byproduct of the divine love, and our immortality is a manifestation of that caring which will never cease to provide for us no matter how much we may reject it. The two immediate practical qualities of love are acceptance and respect for the beloved; the end of that love is transfiguration to the divine nature, but this can alone be achieved according to the consent of the beloved. Threats and coercion can never lead the creature to his destined perfection, since the journey to the Kingdom of God is energized by the power of a free, vibrant will working in fruitful collaboration with the will of God.

The power of God that shone through Jesus brought all

the disciples together in a renewed body, the Body of Christ. Whether in his physical or resurrected form, Jesus was the centre of life and purpose. It is moving to recall the words of Peter when many of Jesus' followers withdrew from his company because of his unacceptably strong teaching. Jesus asked the Twelve whether they too wanted to leave him, and Peter replied, 'Lord, to whom shall we go? Your words are words of eternal life' (John 6:66–88). It is in this context that the statement, 'I am the way; I am the truth and I am life; no one comes to the Father except by me' (John 14:6), is the truth about the Kingdom of God. Only in the personal presence of the Word is the truth of God's nature as Father of all revealed; only in the life of that Word among us is the way to the Kingdom shown. Only in the presence of the Word is life, the life of abundance in God. During the forty days in which Jesus appeared in his disciples in his resurrection body, the body of believers was being fashioned. At that time their amazement must have blossomed into the bliss of recognition, the relief of purpose ending a grey period of disillusionment, of waning hope after so great a promise of glory. They were still limited in their spiritual perspective; they wondered whether Christ intended to establish again the sovereignty of Israel.

And then came the glorious ascension, followed ten days later by the descent of the Holy Spirit on the assembled body of believers. The circumscribed Christ had now departed from their midst to be followed by the assurance of his eternal presence with them from his seat of majesty with the Father. He was no longer available as a person but was universally present as the Lord of life. In the doctrine of the last things, the eschatology in which the terrible advent of God shows itself in a final judgement of the world, there are two strands. One looks to the future, the last day, for the final coming of Christ. This future eschatology has been a glorious, though often terrible, theme running through Holy Scripture since the prophecy of Amos. At that time the children of Israel looked forward to that day as one of final triumph. Amos was the first of many prophets to disabuse the Israelites of their comforting misconception: the day of the Lord was to be one of cosmic darkness, of terror and destruction for them, not one of glorious victory. But with the Christian advent there is another strand, the realized eschatology, which modifies the prophecy of a final judgement without in any way demolishing it.

The theme of this realized cosmic advent of God is proclaimed especially by St Paul in his last letters, believed to have been written in captivity, to the Christians of Colossae and Ephesus. Christ at his resurrection is finally established as the master, not only of the earth, but of the entire universe, as such being in control of the intermediate psychic forces that influence the workings of the world, both externally and internally. His dominion, in one way, was established before the creation of the cosmos – he is the Lamb of God slain before the foundation of the world. This does not only mean that the incarnation and all that followed from it were ordained from the very beginning of the creative act of God, but also that the word, by whom all things are made, is sacrificing himself perpetually in the fecund flowing-forth of life, beauty and love in an essentially indifferent universe. This indifference stems from the selfish attitude of the creature, whether human in our little world or angelic in the vast intermediate realms that energize, and possibly populate, the cosmic spheres. Some of these are tractable to scientific astronomical research, but there are, in addition, in all probability extensive psychic, or astral, realms which the soul explores in its adventures after death until the final coming of the Lord in the future judgement and redemption.

In the wonder of the realized eschatology Christ is with us now, and all who are converted to him in spirit and truth (something rather different from a mere denominational allegiance or a sectarian loyalty) are already living the risen life with him in heaven. This exalted communion with our Lord in heaven is attained during the Eucharist, where in company with the angelic hierarchy and all the host of heaven, we praise God and acknowledge his supreme holiness and his sanctification of the entire universe. In this way we rehearse the awe-inspiring vision that Isaiah had at the beginning of his ministry some seven and a half centuries before Christ (Isaiah 6:1–9). And at that moment the real presence of Christ is available to us as it was to the disciples at the

24

time of the Last Supper. He is always there, but only when we are lifted up to the contemplation of heavenly things can we be available to his constant knocking on the door of our soul. In the same way it is promised that whenever two or three have met together in his name, he is there among them (Matthew 18:20). This is no mere consoling promise but a literal statement of fact: those who are truly gathered in the spirit of Christ enter a dimension of reality that far transcends mere earthly consciousness with its constant interruptions of fear, irritation and disharmony. Those who call on the name of Christ in fervour and dedication are by that very devotion lifted to his presence, and a new world opens for them. Thus they have attained a knowledge of the Kingdom of God at that moment, which is the point of intersection of time and eternity. But, alas, that supreme awareness is evanescent, and almost at once we relapse into the divisive atmosphere of our mundane environment and become imprisoned in a mass of destructive thoughts and attitudes. These impinge on us from the indifferent surroundings where we perform our daily work, but also from the unplumbed depths of our own unconscious lives where cesspits of hatred, resentment and lust lie exposed to the general atmosphere of doubt, selfishness and purpose-lessness that surrounds the world.

All this is very evident from the lives of the early Christian community, as is recorded in the Acts of the Apostles. After the pentecostal experience, the band of rather faint-hearted apostles was cemented into a fellowship that faced constant danger and death with impunity; they knew that even if the body were destroyed, their life in the risen Christ was assured. As St Paul was later to write, 'For to me life is Christ, and death gain; but what if my living on in the body may serve some good purpose? Which then am I to choose? I cannot tell. I am torn two ways: what I should like is to depart and be with Christ; that is better by far; but for your sake there is greater need for me to stay on in the body. This indeed I know for certain: I shall stay, and stand by you all to help you forward and to add joy to your faith, so that when I am with you again, your pride in me may be unbounded in Christ Jesus' (Philippians 1:21–26). Later in the same letter he writes, 'I count everything sheer loss, because all is far outweighed by the gain of knowing Christ Jesus my Lord, for whose sake I did in fact lose everything. I count it so much garbage, for the sake of gaining Christ and finding myself incorporate in him, with no righteousness of my own, no legal rectitude, but the righteousness which comes from faith in Christ, given by God in response to faith. All I care for is to know Christ, to experience the power of his resurrection, and to share his sufferings, in growing conformity with his death, if only I may finally arrive at the resurrection from the dead' (Philippians 3:8–11).

Thus the disciples lived the risen life with Christ in heaven: they shared and they possessed with a common will; they kept nothing back, so that no one had a store of private means that was unavailable to the fellowship. They were so open to God in prayer and to each other in love (the two are complementary, indeed almost synonymous, in terms of the two great commandments of loving God with our whole being and loving our neighbour as ourself) that the Holy Spirit not only infused them with new life but also poured out from them in tumultuous healing power. The gifts of the Holy Spirit enumerated in 1 Corinthians 12 were no mere enthusiastic outpouring of emotional fervour; they were fully-realized phenomena of God's grace constantly renewing a gathering community. The heaven that Adam and Eve had known, albeit without mature cognizance, before they fell into the hell of divisive acquisitiveness was now restored by the resurrection of the Word made flesh and the descent of the Holy Spirit among the earliest disciples. When the power of God infuses the cleansed person – now free from personal striving and an enclosed attitude towards his fellows and indeed towards life itself – the remaking of the entire universe becomes not merely possible but finally inevitable. This later effect is wrought by the transforming power of contemplative prayer that glorifies all it illuminates.

But unfortunately this state of bliss did not persist. The terrible story of Ananias and Sapphira that occurs early in the Acts of the Apostles (5:1–12) tells how soon the germ of private acquisitiveness came to the surface once more. As Adam and Eve could not bear a world of union with God without personal aggrandizement, so the later disciples looked

26

for increasing private gain as a reward for their religious faith. The compromise of service to both God and Mammon soon began to contaminate their devotion. They could see heaven only in terms of acquiring things for themselves. These things included not only money and material possessions but also influence and power. That heaven is its own reward, a doctrine known to all the world's mystics of whatever tradition, was beyond the vision of the later disciples. As the earliest communities became the nuclei of the future churches, as they assumed greater influence in the disintegrating Roman empire, so did political power align itself more definitively to spiritual power. This alliance has always been the bane of spirituality because the lord of this world, identified especially by St John as the devil, seeks to corrupt the faithful. This was, after all, the third temptation presented to Jesus by the devil at the close of his forty-day privation in the wilderness. Jesus resisted because he was filled with the power of God. The later disciples fell, as did Adam and Eve, because they became less aware of the crucified Christ in the face of the attractions of the busy world around them. How to reconcile these opposing forces is the problem of all spiritual life. It is the coming advent of the Lord that alone can effect this healing by the power of his Spirit among us.

4

Christ in You, the Hope of a Glory to Come

It is evident that the advent of Christ in the life of a body of believers, while moving, exalting and transforming in its intensity, is seldom retained for long. The prince of this world seems to have the final word, and the darkness encompasses the light once more almost to the point of eclipsing it. But the light shines on, albeit often in tiny sparks amid the all pervading gloom, testifying to the presence of God in the soul of the individual believer which will not allow itself to be extinguished despite the threat of immediate annihilation. The spirit of mankind is indeed willing, but the flesh, by which we are identified with the world, weighs us down, for we are not to attain spiritual proficiency at the cost of our membership of the incarnate order. A spirituality that lifts us irrevocably above the affairs of the world around us would provide an escape from personal responsibility. It would constitute treason against the material order in which we gain experience and develop mastery. It would find its end in a failure to grow into full humanity, a humanity of divine proportions as evidenced in the life of Christ. Those who have been wonderfully illuminated by the light of the Word constitute the company of saints who are our inspiration and also an unfailing means of communcation with the Holy Spirit.

Those saints of humanity are by no means confined to the visible Christian Church. Many lived centuries before the birth of Christ; we need only to think of the amazing spiritual literature of China and India to see how intensely the ardent human soul was infused with the power of God. At the same time the spiritual evolution of the children of Israel from Moses through to the prophets and sages testifies to the ongoing illumination of the Word lifting up an entire community to levels of spiritual understanding that aspire to a knowledge of God himself. Resisting the exhaustive pressure of materialistic endeavour there breathes the insistent yearning of the soul to a knowledge of reality that moves beyond the attraction of mundane things and will be content with nothing less than the vision of God. As St Augustine learned after a life of intellectual brilliance and sensual profligacy, God has made us for himself alone, and our souls know no rest until they find true rest in him. Tertullian said that the soul was naturally Christian; this in fact is a corollary of the statement in Genesis 1:26–27 that God made man in his own image. It is our privilege to know God directly in mystical union; it is also our splendid enterprise to probe the minutest details of the created order in scientific investigation. But for this union of love and research into truth to be firmly based, the personality has first to be disembarrassed of all selfish aims: it has above all to be cleansed of deceit and emptied of lust. Only then are we so divested of self that the soul is ready to receive the Holy Spirit, as a clean chalice contains the eucharistic wine. Then also can we participate in the great work of knowing God's will and satisfying its demands.

The incarnation of the Word, prefigured so splendidly in the lives of the saints of antiquity, finds its full expression in the life of Christ, who not only gives the authoritative teaching but also initiates the great work of reconciliation in respect of the world and God. By his life he reconciles the sinner to God's grace, for he identifies himself categorically with sin on the cross. Furthermore, that identification is a presage of transfiguration of sin to love, of ashes to beauty. He has a cleansing effect on the personality of everyone who meets him, and the healing work continues unabated when he ascends to heaven and his personal essence is no longer evident to even the inner circle of disciples. It is indeed the change in character and the widening of individual sympathy that testify to the vibrant presence of Christ in the soul, that he is constantly moving the person from self-centred torpor to a dedicated affirmation of life. He comes into his own glory in the lives of all those who welcome his presence – and the first step in such a welcome is acceptance which in turn requires awareness.

It is necessary now to consider some of the spiritual effects of the indwelling Christ on the life of the believer. This is the ever-present life of Christ in the soul, the realized eschatology evidenced in the witness of those who are changed in character. The reality of that change is the renewing effect they have on the world around them, in the lives of those they encounter in their daily work.

The awakening of Christ in the soul, the germination of the seed of the Word into a living, fragile shoot, is accompanied subjectively by an experience of release. The life of the person, previously shut in and occluded by barriers of pride and fear, of resentment and jealousy, is now suddenly wrought open. The Holy Spirit blows in vast draughts of refreshing vitality that raises the soul and lightens the heart of the believer. The personality experiences freedom of an order never previously known, a freedom of sunlit glow and renewing youthfulness. This release effected by the living Christ brings with it a spiritual warmth and an assurance of supernatural love that is independent of the character or past associations of the individual. That one experiences a direct love proves that God, though beyond description and outside all rational categories, has personal attributes, since love is always concerned with the minute particular no less than with the mighty cosmos. To know supernaturally that one is loved means that one is acknowledged as a person, a created being of unique constitution and active, independent will. To be an independently acting person with a will to choose in freedom, in unclouded vision, is a divine quality. It is of God's nature to act in this way. It is no wonder that the Psalmist declares, 'This is my sentence: Gods you may be, sons all of you of a high god, yet you shall die as men die; princes fall, every one of them, and so shall you' (Psalm 82:6–7). If the will is adversely orientated, the downfall of the individual is certain. On the other hand, if the person acts in accordance with divine instruction, his nature approaches that of the Father; as Christ says: those are called gods to whom the word of God is delivered (John 10:34– 35).

The experience of God's unreserved love not only opens the previously locked personality but also shows the way to a purposeful life, to hidden meaning in a previously dark, forbidding world.The purpose in life is seen to be not primarily one of action but of unfolding into spiritual radiance, of being a chalice of divine grace. This is the basis of the assurance of salvation that so often accompanies the advent of Christ in the soul. The soul feels it is saved from damnation and destruction, it is delivered from the temptations of earthly life and the consequences of sinful action; its end is admission to heaven which is indeed experienced, albeit fleetingly, during the moment of realization of God. It shows itself in a radical conversion, or turning about, of the person from the meretricious light of earthly attractions to the uncreated light of God's eternal presence. Salvation is in fact a process of the soul's gradual growth into the light of God's perfect love and it has powerful undertones of healing. In Hinduism and Buddhism the concept of liberation is dominant; it implies the freeing of the individual consciousness from the thraldom of earthly attachments so that it may experience the formless reality of the Godhead. Salvation seems to be a long, arduous spiritual journey in the direction of the more radical renunciation that takes place with liberation. For liberation is closer to the mystical state of union with God than is salvation with its more personal overtones of release, healing and direction to Christ. On the other hand, authentic liberation can be effected only in a soul gradually cleansed of the demands of the ego and open to the full, demanding love of God. This love demands our dedicated service to our fellow creatures, so that our life is no longer entirely our own but is now the life that Christ lives in us.

It is a law of spirituality that no one can see God and remain alive. Even the supreme prophet Moses is allowed to see only God's back when he stands on the rock of Mount Sinai. When God's glory passes by, Moses is put in a crevice of the rock and covered by God's hand. When the hand is removed, Moses is able to see God's back, but God's face is

not to be seen (Exodus 33:21–23). The mystics have some-
times described the supreme experience of the Deity as
dazzling darkness. It is the same darkness that follows a direct
view of the sun; its rays are focused by the eye's lens and
they can easily burn a hole in the retina at the back of the
eye. The result is a darkness that proceeds to total blindness
depending on the intensity of the sun's rays impinging on the
retina. In a similar fashion the full force of God's presence
burns away all that is unclean and impure; only a saint
can bear his presence, and the mystic learns that God is
encountered at the intersection of time and eternity, at the
place of coincidence of opposites: sight and darkness, the void
and the fullness of God's presence, death and immortality.
Thus the experience of salvation that lies at the heart of
Christ's birth in the soul is a pale image of the divine splendour, who is light and in whom there is no darkness at all.
In him our own darkness is burnt away until we can begin
to confront the presence of God, who is best known as *He who
is*. Only as we become more Christlike can we accommodate
the intensity of God's presence in the soul.

This is all of the greatest moment when we consider how
Christ comes to glory in the individual soul. Too often the
first impress of his presence and the openness to the grace of
God that accompanies it is taken by the believer to be an
assurance of total, irrevocable salvation. As a result the
experience is clung to with a fervour that is commendable in
its loyalty but disturbing in its zealous exclusiveness. The
renewal of faith that accompanies the experience of Christ in
the soul brings purpose and meaning with it, a purpose of
individuaal participation in the divine plan of resurrection of
the world and a meaning of triumph in the face of life's uneasy
vicissitudes. Where once there was doubt and distrust there
is now joy and heartwarming hope. But one essential quality
is usually absent: a peace that passes all rational understanding, so that the believer can relax in God and cease to
strive obsessively for others to gain his particular insights so
as to concur absolutely with his view of the divine purpose.
When Christ comes to illuminate our being, we are tempted
to shut down so as to contain his presence within us and to
conserve the power that he bestows on us. If this attitude of

clinging on to his presence persists, we become insidiously entrapped in the very person sent to liberate us. We become imprisoned in a spiritually stultifying outlook based on fear which prevents our further growth into the knowledge of Christ's love and glory.

As in his earthly ministry, Christ issues forth in healing according to the individual's capacity to receive it. While destructive hostility prevents any healing power entering the soul and transforming the person, an attitude of diffidence can also interfere with the work of Christ in the personality by closing the individual to the full impact of the divine presence. If we have misgivings that God's love may be withheld from us because we fail to accept theological statements – as much through ignorance as through a rebellious turn of mind that seeks an understanding faith rather than a merely mechanical repetition of credal formulations – our very uncertainty as to God's displeasure acts to close us to the full thrust of his love. The nature of love is to accept all creatures without reserve; true love, as opposed to affection, has no favourites. Therefore our necessary wariness in accepting dogmatic definition of what are divine mysteries cannot exclude us from God's love. The cry of the distracted parent to Jesus in respect of the healing of his epileptic son, 'I have faith, help me where faith falls short' (Mark 9:24) is a much finer understanding of God's eternal patience and compassion than a deferential acceptance of Christ without the full commitment of the rational soul. It is dialogue that brings us towards a unitive relationship, whether of God or of man, not an awestruck obeisance without any involvement of the thinking and feeling faculties of the inner life. This is one of the many glories of the Psalms; the Psalmist is not afraid to question God's motives and to urge him to move with speed to relieve the trials and indignities of his people. As we ask in a confused medley of perplexity, anxiety, frustration and anger, so God calms us and brings us into a frame of mind where we can hear the silent injunction and be filled with the renewing power of the Holy Spirit.

If love accepts us without discrimination, there are nevertheless some who are more able to respond than others. The criterion of acceptance of the love freely available is our degree of trust that flows out in tenderest innocence. This is the innocence of the little child whom we are urged to become if we are to enter the Kingdom of Heaven. Even if our lives fall far short of childlike innocence, we can attain that blessed state once more by an act of recollection, repentance and confession. As we read in 1 John 1:8–9, if we claim to be sinless, we are self-deceived and strangers to the truth. If we confess our sins, he is just and may be trusted to forgive our sins and cleanse us from every kind of wrong. Once we are so cleansed and our will is committed to an amendment of our way of life, we attain a state of primal innocence once more, and can start to lead a new life. Unfortunately, the will to change is weak in most of us, and repeated falls from virtue may be inevitable before the full flowering of the seed of Christ takes place within the soul. By contrast, there is the constitutionally evil person, whose presence in any society is not to be explained away purely in sociological or psychological terms, for his darkness is much more inveterate than mere superficial mechanisms of degradation. Such an individual is so full of his own darkness that there is no place in his personality for the downpouring of God's love. His scheme and destiny in the cosmos is one of the enigmas of creation and an everpresent mystery in the redemption of the world in Christ.

A fanatical devotion to any object of belief, even to Christ himself, is often energized by a fear of life that is deeply rooted in the unconscious depths of the mind. This fear of life is based on an inner insecurity: if we betray the object of devotion, some dreadful misfortune will assail us. And so the devotion is sustained with grim determination for the sake of an untroubled existence. The devotion becomes quite literally a matter of life and death in the mind of the neurotically obsessive believer. In this obsessively clinging encounter – it barely merits the designation of fellowship – the nature of the Word is obscured. Christ becomes less a person of love and release and more a bulwark against the shadowy elements of mortal life. And yet it is in the experience of the shadow side of life and our own personality that we grow progressively into mature beings, ultimately to be measured by nothing less than the full stature of Christ, as St Paul writes in Ephesians

4:13. The more we cling to past images, and the more we look towards our own safety, the further we distance ourselves from a knowledge of God. As a sequel to this we separate ourselves increasingly from the fellowship of God and man that heralds our own transformation into children of light.

Once Christ becomes a magical protection against the misfortunes germane to our mortal existence, our system of belief subtly replaces God in our lives. Then whoever appears to challenge that rigid system is identified with the powers of darkness. The end is a rejection of a large mass of humanity and our encapsulation in a limited group who hold unswervingly to our beliefs. In such a self-righteous, glibly complacent company there is little opportunity for the growth of the soul into greater spiritual truth. In fact the complacency of such a group is merely superficial, for deeper down there is an intolerable uncertainty that gnaws away at the imposing superstructure of the edifice of faith so painstakingly erected and so heavily buttressed. It attempts to define an absolute line of demarcation between the saved and unsaved, yet no one can be absolutely sure on which side of the line he stands. Salvation may indeed come to us as a dramatic experience of God's love in the soul, but its full impact in our lives is a slow, painful process. 'Up to the present, we know, the whole created universe groans in all its parts as if in the pangs of childbirth. Not only so, but even we, to whom the Spirit is given as firstfruits of the harvest to come, are groaning inwardly while we wait for God to make us his sons and set our whole body free. For we have been saved, though only in hope. Now to see is no longer to hope: why should a man endure and wait for what he already sees? But if we hope for something we do not yet see, then, in waiting for it, we show our endurance'(Romans 8:22–25). It is the development of this hope into clear, unobstructed vision that is the measure of Christ's coming in glory in our lives.

Once Christ has revealed his presence in the soul and has discharged the pall of doubt that clouds our vision and dulls our spiritual aspiration, he paradoxically leads us away from the light of assurance into the darkness of self-discovery. His light first inspires us with hope and meaning, but this is merely a preliminary to the inner cleansing work that the

Holy Spirit has to perform. When Jesus was baptized and the Spirit dwelt definitively in him, that same Spirit led him into the wilderness to be tempted by the prince of darkness who subverts our material existence. So likewise the Spirit leads us into the depth of the soul, there to confront our personal failings, especially lust for power, resentment, jealousy and avarice. This is at least as authentic a work of the Holy Spirit as are the more spectacular charismatic phenomena that tend to be especially coveted by those who are young in the spiritual life – no doubt a reflection of their own deeper uncertainty. Charismatic powers in the absence of a purified inner life are very likely to do later damage after bestowing an initial, transitory blessing on both the individuals exhibiting them and those receiving them. It is in this context a greater spiritual attainment to weep spontaneously for our sins that to work exceptional miracles. In the act of humble contrition the soul is cleansed of much rubbish; after the period of tears it is able to accommodate the profligacy of God's love. After the rigour of the judgement comes the glowing warmth of God's unlimited forgiveness, the flow of heavenly grace. On the other hand, the working of unusual phenomena tends to exalt the ego often at the expense of a deeper knowledge of God, and these are better avoided until the person is sufficiently humble to be able to give unrestrained glory to God. In Jesus' parable it was the worthless publican who was justified, who came into right relationship with God – once he had acknowledged that he had nothing to offer except his sinful nature – rather than the Pharisee who interposed his own virtue between himself and God. The publican gave himself, unworthy as he was, whereas the Pharisee gave nothing of himself, but merely exulted in his gifts, at the same time despising other people. In the same way, miracle workers can easily believe in their special dispensation to the subtle exclusion of the One from whom all good works proceed. This is a hazard in the lives of all those who exhibit special gifts: self-glorification supersedes the work of transformation and inner renewal.

All this again stresses that the coming of Christ in glory in the soul is a slow process, progressive in its healing action and thorough in its capacity to change the perspective of the individual from mere self-interest to self-sacrifice on behalf of the world. We are, however, often very impatient: we look for external signs of power while averting our gaze from the revelations of inner disorder. While there is even a trace of self-seeking within us, one spark of aversion towards our neighbour, the work of inner cleansing has to proceed. Furthermore, as we proceed along the inner path of purgation, so do shafts of gluttony, lust, jealousy and resentment suddenly erupt to the exterior. Thesee embarrassments help to show us the vast distance we have to traverse before we attain a full dedication to Christ in our midst. The value of this descent into our private cesspit of corruption is that, as its foul contents are brought to the light of spiritual discernment, so we attain an empathy with our fellow men that is overwhelming in intensity, not merely an intellectual abstraction. As Christ mixed with the common people in their thoughtless degradation, so we too have to come to terms with the gamut of disturbance within our own personality and in turn with the disturbance common to humanity. In the Parable of the Publican and the Pharisee, the publican could attain that relationship with his peers – and indeed all people – by virtue of his own humility. The Pharisee, by contrast, had so separated himself by his own imagined excellence from his peers that he could not relate authentically either to God or to man.

In the same way, the mother of Jesus was so empty of guile and thoughts of self-importance that she was able to contain the fruit of the Holy Spirit within her soul – of which the womb was an external reflection. When Christ comes in glory into the individual soul – which is at the same time in corporate unity with the universal soul of life – he not only cleanses it of its accumulated dross, but acts to transmute that very dross into a fabric of purity to embellish the newly-born individual. Humility is the ultimate virtue of the spiritual life; it keeps us young in spirit as we are enabled to learn from even the most unprepossessing of our brethren. Jesus is our exemplar in humility; as he taught the common people, so he learned from them the secrets of human existence, both degraded and heroic. The light of righteousness burns inextinguishably in the untroubled atmosphere of humility until the whole world is bathed in the splendour of its radiance. Such a light illumines the purified soul, making it a fit receptacle for the gifts of God and the fruits of his Spirit. This is the work of Christ in the soul, and its love, joy and peace enrich the lives of all who encounter it in the day's work. So too did Jesus enrich all those who were open to his love.

5

The Marks of Christ
(1) Freedom and Detachment

The life in Christ, in common with other spiritual paths, tends to extremes of zeal on the one hand and worldliness on the other. In the formative period the spirit of dedication so grips the disciple that life is made meaningful only by a knowledge of the Lord, while death is unimportant except that it brings closer the day of universal consummation of all things in God. The letters to the seven churches in Asia that prefix the Book of Revelation underline the principal snares in the path of discipleship. Some, like the congregations of Pergamum and Thyatira, are liable to seduction by esoteric cults and gnostic philosophies, while others, like the church of Ephesus, succeed in holding on to the faith but with a growing hardness of heart that shuts out love. Yet others, like the churches of Sardis and Laodicea, lapse into a torpor that precludes spiritual development, even if, in the instance of Laodicea, there is a complacent pride in its self-sufficiency which is mistakenly equated with spiritual distinction. To balance those aberrations, however, there flickers the light of a true undefiled faith burning painfully through the darkness of persecution, as in the churches of Smyrna and Philadelphia.

On one level the call of Christ in the soul is to a more perfect way of life. Malice, lust, jealousy and sloth are to be replaced by compassion, chastity, charity and unremitting service to others. And yet the teaching of Jesus and his way of life among his fellows moved positively in the direction of acceptance, tolerance of human weakness, and a charter of personal freedom far in advance of the religious orthodoxy of his own time, and indeed of the rules and regulations of all societies at any time. When Christ makes his presence felt in the soul of the earnest seeker after truth, that disciple may be so uplifted as to feel he is 'born again' in the faith, as opposed to the rather perfunctory religion he learned at home and later as part of his academic equipment. He may be tempted to recoil in horror from his past attitudes and general style of life Now at last he has found the true faith, in the process of which he unceremoniously kicks away the ladder of his life on which he ascended so painfully to his present situation of faith. In his limited but enthusiastic view the past was a complete aberration, while the present situation represents the final destination to which he has been guided so miraculously. In this way the supercilious worldliness of the Laodicean situation is replaced by the loveless eartnestness of the church of the Ephesians. In more modern times there have been episodes of religious revival, and nearly all of these have followed hard on a particularly arid period of intellectual enlightenment or a phase of moral permissiveness. This sequence itself testifies to the spiritually barren world of intellectual speculation, scientific research, social experimentation and sensual stimulation in the absence of a living faith. These other modes of human actualization, important as they may be on a purely practical level, are all impaled on the spikes of transience, decay and dissolution. They do not inflame the soul with that joy of recognition which may suddenly dawn after the unexpected meeting with a stranger that opens the previously sluggish eyes of the soul to a vision of eternity.

Indeed, man does not live by bread alone, but by every word that proceeds from the mouth of God. This word is the bread of life, and to taste and eat it is to be raised up from the imprisonment of earthly life to a vision of eternity. The misfortune lies in the human tendency to secrete the bread of life so that it may assume the function of an infallible source of reassurance instead of performing its vital work of guiding the spirit into new realms of understanding and healing. Christ did not come into the world to provide a bastion against suffering, disappointment and death. In his earthly life he experienced the full gamut of the world's pain and suffering, and was not miraculously delivered from any of them. But he had the inner strength to persist so that finally he not only prevailed but was found fully worthy of a complete resurrection to eternal life. No element of his personality was found wanting. The true life of the spirit is not one that leads to a limitation, still less a denial, of the faculties of the personality. There has to be an uninhibited encounter with the world's many snares and illusions that bear down upon the human psyche. The spiritual life is one of active participation in all aspects of earthly existence, vibrant yet terrifying in its glory and agony minute by minute. In this sharing we learn from each experience and encounter. In turn we contribute our essence to the world's atmosphere, so that both the world and the individual are thereby enriched. In other words, it is our privilege to enjoy each moment of life and our responsibility to bear the Holy Spirit to all who receive us and to share the grace of God that flows from us.

It is sad and an eloquent indication of our imperfect scale of values that the concept of orthodoxy in religion carries with it undertones of dreariness, intolerance and general curtailment of human potential. To many people orthodox religion is joyless, obsessed with the fact of evil and the need to protect oneself against its inroads at any price, and generally divisive in terms of human relationships. Between the saved and the unsaved, the elect and those beyond the pale, there is a wide gulf without any obvious bridge joining the two sides. The object of life is to keep strenuously on the right side of the barrier, so that in the end human relationships are restricted to a small body of believers. Yet to be fair, it must be conceded that free, uninhibited social intercourse does bring with it the hazard of contamination with undesirable forces that may damage the intellect and poison the soul. All this is painfully shown in the sacred history of the Jews; it is only in Christ that a way is shown to bridge this gulf without in any way denying the difficulties involved.

From the time of its definitive election as a chosen people under Moses, the children of Israel were entrusted with an elaborate code of moral and ritual behaviour which they were forbidden to contravene. Especially important was religious observance and the social obligations that flow out from it. The Ten Commandments were the distillation of that vast body of doctrine: even today their authority has not been undermined in the lives of civilized people even if they are being constantly betrayed by most people, even sincere believers: the spirit is willing but the flesh weak. The children of Israel were indeed God's chosen people, chosen to reveal his sacred law to the world, to witness to that Law by becoming holy, a nation of priests set apart to intercede between man and God. Nevertheless, when they reached the promised land, they almost immediately apostasized. Forgetting their debt to God, they allowed themselves to be seduced by the world around them and especially the cults of their pagan neighbours. Each period of backsliding brought in its wake military disaster, enslavement by their ignorant, depraved neighbours, a spirit of sincere, though selfish, repentance, and the emergence, through God's grace, of a national, religious leader. He brought the broken, penitent Israelites to victory, but their gratitude to God was shortlived. Peace and freedom brought complacency to the fore again, and the ensuing period of moral decline culminated once more in open apostasy. This dismal pattern of events recurred until the disappearance of the northern kingdom of Israel into Assyrian captivity in the eighth century before Christ, and the deportation into Babylonian exile of the southern kingdom of Judah. This culminated in the sacking of Jerusalem and the destruction of the temple in 587 BC. Perhaps the most significant example of the cause of this trend is evidenced in the fall from spiritual dedication of Solomon. His reign marked the culmination of national splendour, while his wisdom was to be proverbial in its reach and profundity. His downfall was women; promiscuous relationships with those around him, Israelite and pagan according to his lust, served to dilute his religious fervour and corrupt his moral discernment. He offered worship to local deities to please his pagan wives and concubines, thereby placing these idols on the same level as God himself. Solomon's reign marked both the zenith of Israelite power and also its insidious decline towards schism, defeat, deportation and death.

When, through the magnanimity of Cyrus, king of Persia,

the exiles were allowed to return to Palestine once more, a chastened people emerged who were to form the nucleus of Judaism. Under Ezra and Nehemiah the temple was rebuilt and the walls of Jerusalem were repaired. Then came the final edict: all mixed marriages were to be dissolved. From that time onwards a racially pure people were alone to be tolerated. The snares of religious syncretism and the debased psychic and physical practices of the pagan groups were to be excluded from the orbit of God's chosen people. At last the prophetic injunction could be fulfilled: you shall be my people, and I shall be your God. But no one can immure himself permanently from the world's insistent call to full participation in its workings. In fact Judaism gained much from the insights of Persian religion as it was subsequently to do from its encounter with Hellenism after Alexander the Great won control of the hinterland of Palestine among his greater conquests. While complete segregation was enjoined by the highly orthodox strand, a more universalist approach in Judaism was also apparent in the books of Ruth and especially Jonah that were written at about the same time as the edicts of Ezra and Nehemiah. On the whole the Jewish people remained pure through the period of the Maccabean revolt up to the time of Christ. It seems appropriate that the incarnation should have taken place among an essentially pure, committed group of people, though the genealogy of Jesus according to Matthew's account traces the line of descent from four non-Israelite women in addition to the remainder who were Jewish; the non-Israelites were Tamar, Rahab, Ruth and Bathsheba.

In Christ a new relationship is present with the world; there is neither fear of contamination nor the danger of capitulation to its debased values. Instead, there is an active, fully willed participation in all its activities and among the most degraded people, with whom the Lord of life has no difficulty in identifying himself. He can achieve this wholehearted identification because he has established his own incontrovertible identity. Indeed, he comes to call the sinner to repentance and the sick to be healed. Those who pride themselves on their health, whether bodily or spiritual, are the ones most in need of a doctor of souls, but they cannot receive Christ because they are closed to a deep knowledge of themselves and consequently cannot respond to the call of God beyond them. Where there is no contact with the soul within, there does evil dwell. It is not so much the superficially sinful person who is the greatest repository of evil forces, because he is at least open to love which alone can deal constructively with the darkness of evil. He is more often the outwardly virtuous person who is devoid of charity that has a closed heart – a heart of stone as Ezekiel would describe it – and a personality emanating forces of hatred and darkness. This was apparently the situation of the church at Ephesus, and is very common in revivalist groups. These are strong in their own special brand of faith, but closed to the impulse of love and forgiveness. Their state of spiritual imprisonment is usually due to an amalgam of resentment and fear. The resentment follows the apparent worldly success of sinners, and their fear is due to the menace of evil which they rightly sense but whose origin within themselves they cannot trace. In fact evil is cosmic in scope, but it finds an especially welcome home in all those who are susceptible to its thrust. These include the power-seekers, the emotionally unbalanced who look for relief in sex, drugs and the pursuit of occult practices, and the tight-lipped fanatics who will not yield their limited vision of truth to any possibility of extension.

That person is free who can be fully himself in all situations, needing neither to impress the important members of society nor ingratiate the poor. We can be free only when we can operate from a fixed centre of indentity within ourselves. Even if we are only on the first rungs of the spiritual ladder and our centre responds most positively to sensual pleasure, money or worldly power, our identity is becoming established, though its aims are not praiseworthy. The tax-gatherers, prostitutes and other despised members of the society which Jesus frequented were centred on this lower rung of identity and could be authentically themselves albeit offensive to their fellows because of their squalid livelihood. They were free to respond to his holiness by ascending the spiritual ladder. And so their subservience to the attractions of this world was overcome until they could find their true place only at the heavenly banquet presided over by Christ himself. At that juncture they were free of all worldly encumbrances, and could give of themselves without stint to all who called on their help.

The more fully Christ is incarnated in the soul, the closer becomes the bond between the personality of the believer and his compatriots, between himself and God.

This God no longer needs to be bribed, placated or obsequiously praised. He becomes less separate from us as he is incarnated more perfectly within us. The statement of John 10:30 that the Father and Christ are one becomes more true of the individual soul as the Word grows more perfectly into the tree of life within it. Freedom brings trust with it so that we can rest with assurance in God's love. He is recognized at last as not fickle, vengeful or punitive. He is all-loving, and as we know him more perfectly, so love infuses our very being, changing us into new people. This love seeks nothing outside itself since it embraces everything. Its possession is each moment in time as life passes in the endless stream of eternity. It has no reward except its constant effect in bringing everything it encounters to the peak of its own perfection. Whenever there is a motive behind our benevolence we may be sure that our love is imperfect, that we are barely started on our spiritual career. There is in fact only one proper motive in loving someone, and that is to bring him to that freedom to be himself that is a measure of God's presence within him.

In this spiritual freedom we need no longer fear psychic contamination, nor, on the other hand, do we seek after esoteric knowledge to substantiate our frail self-regard. We are no longer subject to the claims of opposing systems of thought, for they cannot blur our inner vision of the one God who transcends all intellectual barriers and racial divisions. Nor are we attached to the riches of this world, any more than having to turn our backs conspicuously upon them lest they ensnare us. Neither wealth nor its absence will bring us to the vision of God but only a proper use of the world's resources, for all who live among us. It is for this reason that spiritual truth can be enunciated most convincingly in paradox; that which is logically absurd on the level of the rational mind becomes a deep abiding truth when viewed spiritually. What the discursive intellect grasps, analyses and destroys is taken up by the wisdom of the Holy Spirit and brought into a context far beyond the limitations of time and space, in a realm in which all opposites are reconciled, all contradictions coincide. This is the exceptional work of love. He who loves one person in this way loves all life. Love is above the corrupting influence of the power-inflated dema-gogue and intellectually fluent theorist who would seek to destroy anything that contradicted them, thereby threatening their supremacy.

'Where the Spirit of the Lord is, there is liberty' (2 Corin-thians 3:17). This Spirit is also one that issues forth in charismatic phenomena, but until these are illumined in a supernatural love, they are as liable to be self-inflating as healing, disruptive of relationships as reconciling all things to God. True liberty, the freedom of the Spirit that issues from the Word in the soul, is one in which we speak and act from the soul, which is the true focus of our identity. In that state of release, the ego consciousness by which we effect communication with the world around us and do the work we are to perform with efficiency, is in full alignment with the soul, which in turn is fully open to God in Christ. It is then that our presence brings the light of God on to all whom we meet, setting them free from the limitations of their own background and bringing them into universal relationship with all the elements of life. When Adam and Eve lived in unconscious harmony with God's universe, they were free to be themselves and they knew no shame in their nakedness. As soon as they followed their own selfish devices and fell from the unitive knowledge of God, their freedom waned so that even their previously innocent bodies were a stumbling-block that had to be covered in confusion. When Christ is restored to the soul as a living presence and not merely a remote principle, we return to that primal innocence in which we can show ourselves in our nakedness to all the world. We have nothing shameful to conceal; all we have is available to anyone who needs it. 'Come to me, all whose work is hard, whose load is heavy; and I will give you relief' (Matthew 11:28). The welcoming words of Christ come with greatest conviction from the souls of all who are freed from attachment to possessions, and can give of themselves in their simplicity to others.

It is thus that the statement of Christ is best understood, that the person who cannot receive the Kingdom of God as a little child, will be unable to enter it. That simplicity of a young child, the prerequisite for the heavenly life, comes to those who are released from all worldly attachments and can give their whole attention freely to the moment in hand. They give because it is the nature of love to be freely available; renunciation is the way to God in Christ. They give of themselves to all who will receive them; they demand no personal allegiance, for the life they live is no longer a private, self-centred domain but one in which Christ is the directive power so that all the person's gifts are dedicated in turn to him. The firstfruit of the living Christ, both personal and communal, is a radical loosening from past attachments, whether material possessions, national pride or stifling personal relationships they lead neither party to freedom, and are terminated tragically by death.

In the story of the rich young man who sought eternal life Jesus could see that in this instance there was a strong attachment to wealth. This interfered with his participation in life and kept him back from the ultimate commitment to God. This is an invariable effect of possessing large amounts of this world's goods: too much valuable attention is squandered on their maintenance and investment, so that too little time is left for the Kingdom of God and his creation. Indeed, it is impossible to serve God and money with equal devotion. One way of resolving the conflict is to dispense completely with all worldly goods, but an even more satisfactory solution is to act as a faithful steward of the world's resources while at the same time dedicating oneself to the service of God and one's fellow creatures in prayer, social action and love. In this way our service is to God, and its fruit is the raising up to spiritual radiance of everything we encounter in a day's work. When we are free in Christ, we can handle the world's produce with reverence and joy without yielding to the temptation of possessing it.

The joy of the freedom to which detachment witnesses is particularly well seen in relation to a priceless work of art.

When we are attached to the things of this world we covet such a masterpiece not only because of its financial value, but also for the distinction its possession affords us. But as we gloat over the work of art in private, so does its beauty begin to pall until both we and it are subtly imprisoned in a web of illusion, the illusion of personal possession. We possess it materially as it possesses us spiritually. As we secrete it from the world so does it separate us insidiously from other people until much of our concern is centred on its preservation. But once it is donated to the world, its beauty becomes universally available and we are free to enjoy it in the company of other people. We make the important discovery that beauty shared in public has a higher aesthetic appeal than that which is enjoyed privately. The reason for this is that the intrinsic beauty of a work of art is spiritually enhanced by the joy of recognition evinced in those who appreciate it. In the same way a memorable concert has an inspiring effect that even a very fine musical recording lacks. Likewise, when we are free we can enjoy life to the full without clinging on to it. In this way it is no longer darkened by the threat of finitude, ageing or death.

Human relationships likewise attain their peak when all involved are free in themselves. In that freedom they do not need another person's company, with the result that their relations are spontaneous, sincere and fulfilling. They can end a conversation at will without either feeling embarrassed or evincing disapproval of the other person. When Christ is alive in the soul we forfeit our sense of competence and mastery that separates us from our fellows, but instead we donate our gifts to them, at the same time effecting a deep identification with them. He who would live in imitation of Christ must aspire not to world-transcending spiritual authority, but to the deepest humility: the resurrection commenced on the cross when Jesus held out his arms wide in forgiveness and reconciliation to the whole world. Even today after twenty centuries the world has scarcely understood the offer he made to it, but the invitation to enter the heavenly Kingdom still stands open.

Freedom brings with it patience, for even in the waiting there is communion with the heavenly Kingdom. To sit waiting for an appointment that is unexpectedly delayed provides an excellent opportunity to open oneself to the moment in hand, and so enter a dimension of reality where there is peace and acceptance. All our impatience cannot alter the course of an immutable event, but if we can offer the time up to God, he brings us up to himself and we discover that fruition can take place even in the silence of standing still and waiting. In this stillness we learn the importance and practice of awareness, an essential requirement as we await Christ's full coming in glory, his parousia, at the end of time.

6

The Marks of Christ
(2) Commitment and Reconciliation

As the living Christ establishes himself more completely in the soul, so does a measure of self-confidence show itself that is of another order to the self-inflation that worldly powers confer. While our self-awareness is limited to money, social position (or the lack of it), intellectual brilliance or artistic gifts, it will continue to be in a state of flux. It will balance uneasily in the world of changing values, of vogue attachments that disappear as suddenly as they first arose. When we retire from the active demands of the world and can rest in our own being, we can begin to assess what we have really made of our lives. If this assessment is linked to outer achievements, we will soon discover how vain our course has been. Others who succeed us seem to supplant our efforts, and even if we achieve renown at one time, soon our contribution becomes a mere footnote in the annals of history, if indeed it is remembered at all. Montaigne says, 'Fame and tranquillity can never be bedfellows', and he is right on a number of different levels. Fame brings with it unease lest we are superseded by others on the same ladder that we have ascended. It also brings many inquirers and would-be followers, even disciples to the master, and most of these disturb his peace with their problems of personality. Reading between the lines of the Gospels, one can see how often the incomprehension and self-seeking of the apostles must have irritated Jesus. Their obtuseness was exposed all too starkly at the time of his passion, when they ran away from the one who had nourished them spiritually at great cost to himself. While fame seeks for itself, it can know no peace. But when it gives itself to God, it becomes a bastion that can afford support – albeit temporarily – to many people. Finally they have to relinquish that protection and venture on into the world alone, but now the influence of their master acts as a spur to their further efforts. Thus when the resurrected Christ finally ascends in mystical union to the Father, he sends down the Holy Spirit to inspire the disciples to continue in the work that he initiated while with them in the flesh.

The confirmation of the self, which is the essence of authentic self-confidence, that Christ bestows inculcates a scale of values and indicates a way of life that lead the disciple beyond concern for his prestige to a commitment in love to the whole world. He no longer is interested in his own safety, for he knows dimly yet incontestably that his authentic nature is eternal. The statement of Christ, reiterated in the mystical tradition generally, that the man who seeks his life will lose it, but he who gives up his very life for God, will find eternal life, is proved in the experience of those who tread the spiritual path. This path, as has already been noted, is not one of unimpeded, glorious ascent to the Deity in which all conflicting elements in the personality are conveniently shed. It is one that traverses the darkness of the unconscious, both personal and collective (the two are in fact facets of the same modality, just as the microcosm mirrors the macrocosm), so that the total darkness may be infused with light and enter transfigured into the divine realm. In the divine economy nothing is too mean for salvation, no element of creation is wasted. This is the self-confidence that can never be shaken for it knows that the person is loved for himself alone as part of the love God has for all his creatures. This self-confidence is conferred by the presence of Christ within, so that, as St Paul puts it so concisely in Galatians 2:20, after we have been crucified with him the life we live is no longer our own life, but the life that Christ lives in us. The necessity for prior crucifixion is important: until the past selfish existence is repudiated, a circumstance that usually follows dramatic misfortune of one type or another, Christ cannot get near us

– or, to put it another way, his seed cannot germinate in the soul.

When we know Christ in the soul as both a principle and a personal presence that directs us to an encounter with God, our allegiance to him cannot fail to be total. When Peter on three occasions during the period of the betrayal denied so much as knowing Jesus, he was speaking more truly than he knew. To be sure he knew the man well enough, though fear for his own life bade him disclaim any relationship with Jesus. But of the deeper Christ in the heart, who both directs our life and fills it with universal compassion, he knew nothing. The crucifixion and all that followed it up to his own eventual martyrdom were to bring the true knowledge of Christ as a living presence within him. When we are committed to Christ, the life of Christ is our pattern and our hope. For the truth we are prepared to give up our very life, since there can be no compromise with ultimate values. We read in Deuteronomy 30:19, 'I summon heaven and earth to witness against you this day: I offer you the choice of life or death, blessing or curse. Choose life . . . ' There can be no double set of values in creation: the way of God leads to life abundant, whereas its antithesis produces a general deterioration that ends in chaos, a state of negation that returns to the non-existence before God created the cosmos.

Commitment to Christ is the ultimate purpose of life. It should be envisaged primarily as allegiance to the values that Jesus inculcated and bore witness to in his ministry among us. Later on, the knowledge of a divine saviour becomes more insistent in the soul. This path of unfolding is preferable to one of great personal devotion to Jesus without a growth in sanctity and love of the whole person. It might be argued that the general spiritualization of the person is impossible without a prior dedication of oneself to Christ, but as Jesus himself remarked to the woman who praised him rapturously, blessing the womb that had carried him and the breasts that had suckled him, 'No, happy are those who hear the word of God and keep it' (Luke 11:27–28). The true Christ illuminates the soul and transforms the personality; his presence is known by its effect not by its claim for recognition. The personal saviour points the way to the Father, a way illuminated by the Holy Spirit. 'I am the way; I am the truth and I am life; no one comes to the Father except by me' (John 14:6). He is the light of the universe as well as the light of the individual soul; by his light we too become the light of our little world. Ultimately the collective witness of a sanctified humanity acts as a transfiguring light of the world, so that it passes beyond corruption to eternal life.

That light, which shows itself in our personal lives as the peak of conscience which will never allow us to rest until we have fulfilled its extreme demand, is the focus of our commitment to God. This ultimate demand is summed up in the law of holiness: 'You shall be holy, because I, the Lord your God, am holy' (Leviticus 19:2). As long as we evade that ultimate charge, we will have betrayed the high calling of humanity, a calling definitively obeyed and manifested in the life of Jesus. It is in that life that we can identify the man with the principle of holiness that inhabits the peak of the soul. This sacred point is known as the apex of the soul, alternatively as its ground (base) or its centre; in mystical psychology all words with a spatial connotation must be seen as metaphors pointing to a reality as ineffable as God himself. As we read in Hebrews 10:31, it is a terrible thing to fall into the hands of the living God. This applies especially after we have been shown the definitive truth and have deliberately turned away from it to follow a lesser path. It is not the grandeur of our work in the world that counts; what forms the basis of our future judgement is how we respond to the demands of integrity in the course of that work.

Commitment therefore follows the categorical command of Christ in the soul to fulfil the responsibilities that our humanity, as evidenced in the life of Jesus, imposes on us. We may be tempted by the prince of this world, as Jesus was throughout his life from the moment of his baptism until he breathed his last on the cross, but we will never be seduced from our high calling. The first part of Jesus' temptation was towards self-aggrandizement because of the magnitude of his spiritual gifts; the last part moved towards despair in the face of impenetrable psychic darkness. It was his closeness to his Father, especially near, paradoxically, when God seemed most remote to him on the cross and he cried out, 'My God, my God, why hast thou forsaken me?' that determined his victory over darkness and his unique resurrection from the dead. That closeness to God was effected on a practical level by unfailing prayer, as much when all was going well as when he was suffering in inarticulate agony. A person who knows Christ intimately as a soul presence throughout the vicissitudes of this mortal life can never be seduced by worldly things or competing spiritual philosophies. Indeed, in his presence all the apparatus of the intellect is stunned into silence: 'But the Lord is in his holy temple; let all the earth be hushed in his presence' (Habakkuk 2:20).

True commitment, again paradoxically, brings with it tolerance, moderation in our relationship with all people, and an ecumenism that is of a different order to a rootless, spineless syncretism that sees all forms as virtually the same and can therefore borrow indiscriminately from them to fashion a hybrid religion. St Paul writes in Philippians 4:4–7, 'I wish you all joy in the Lord. I will say it again: all joy be yours. Let your magnanimity be manifest to all. The Lord is near; have no anxiety, but in everything make your requests known to God in prayer and petition with thanksgiving. Then the peace of God, which is beyond our utmost understanding, will keep guard over your hearts and your thoughts, in Christ Jesus.' When we are rooted in God, and Christ has grown in the soul to the stature of a mighty tree, we can flow out in disinterested love to the whole creation. This includes especially our fellow human beings who may have opinions and religious views very different from our own and whose lifestyle may likewise contravene the canons of propriety that we had long accepted without deliberation. This love accepts people for what they are, so that they cease to threaten us by their own cultural background and mode of religious observance. Jesus speaks about the person who hears his words and acts upon them as one who can resist all the threats and hazards of the world, because the foundation of his spiritual edifice is composed of rock, indeed the rock of ages who is God himself. Such a person is so secure in his own identity that he can listen with courtesy to all he hears from alien sources. Some he will reject because it contravenes the law of Christ within, which is love; some he will accept with gratitude inasmuch as it sheds light on obscure areas of his own traditions so that he can understand it better; some he will retain tentatively in the back of his mind for future consideration when he may be more competent to judge the validity of the propostions propounded. The essential strength, however, is that the free person can inspect all assertions and philosophies with a warmth of regard that will tend to bring their numerous protagonists into his loving presence where they may experience the living Christ. They will know him in his daily work of healing reconciliation.

The highest point in the religious vocation is this work of reconciliation. Reconciliation is indeed even more holy than ecumenism, because it follows the clauses in the prayer of St Francis, 'Lord, make me an instrument of your peace; where there is hatred, let me sow love; where there is injury, pardon'. The one who repents of the sins he or his group have committed in the past by now offering himself as a sacrifice to those who have been hurt has surmounted one rung of the ladder of reconciliation. An even higher rung is attained by those who have been fearfully hurt in the past, then visiting their erstwhile despoilers in love and forgiveness. Those who, for instance, suffered terribly under the Nazi cruelty, but could, after hostilities had ended, go back to the countries where they had been tortured and spread the light of Christ – a light that far transcends denominational barriers, being as radiant in Jews like Martin Buber and Leo Baeck or Hindus like Mahatma Gandhi or Sri Ramana Maharshi as in any contemporary Christian saint – are among the ultimate instruments of human reconciliation. In Jesus, in whom the human and divine natures coinhere in equality, both these rungs of reconciliation are attained and integrated; he gave up his life for the world, and he reappeared in love at the time of his resurrection to those who had repudiated him when he lay tortured and disfigured by those who hated him. St Paul saw truly when he wrote, 'God was in Christ reconciling the world to himself' (2 Corinthians 5:19).

Ecumenism works towards the breaking-down of denominational barriers, but it tends to be limited by theological considerations. As far as it goes it is admirable, but by its very nature it is cautious and tentative. Reconciliation, on the other hand, is headstrong and self-sacrificing – indeed, the only self it recognizes is the spirit of love which gives up its life impetuously for its friend, who is every man. This reconciliation is possible only for the person whose soul is unreservedly open to love. Alternatively we might say that he has greatness of heart, that the centre of his personality has moved inwards from the head with its cool, discriminatory acquiescence to the heart with its warmth and impulsive acceptance. This passionate welcome finds its paradigm in the response of the father to the return home of his penitent son in the Parable of the Prodigal Son. This parable assures us of God's unreserved acceptance whether in this world or the life after death when we come to him in penitence and faith. The growth of Christ in the soul leads to the development and unfolding of the heart; the heart can accommodate all things provisionally. The magnanimity that Paul speaks about in the Letter to the Philippians follows a resting of the entire personality in the providence of God, in the abundant love of Christ.

This movement of the seat of spiritual consciousness from the head with its intellectual analysis to the heart with its glowing welcome, 'Come to me, all whose work is hard, whose load is heavy; and I will give you relief' (Matthew 11:28), is effected not so much by prayer techniques as by the passionate response of the soul to the many and varied episodes of common life. When Jesus saw the people around him with their diseases and emotional burdens, he was moved with compassion. That compassion opened him wide to his Father as well as to the people in their need. He could take the suffering multitude into his heart and heal them when they were willing. 'O Jerusalem, Jerusalem . . . how often have I longed to gather your children, as a hen gathers her brood under her wings; but you would not let me' (Matthew 23:37).

When one is in the company of such a person of the heart, one's own heart opens in sympathy that culminates in a response of trust and dedication to the Most High. I personally have known a number of such heart-directed people in my life. One was a Russian Orthodox ecumenist of radiant love who was shortly to die. His sight was so defective that he could not see me directly, but we saw clearly into the depths of each other's souls. We exchanged individual insights about the phenomenon of death and the principle within us that proceeds into the life of the world to come. When he died he was closer to me even than when he was still in the flesh. Another man of the heart was an Anglican monk whose apparent eccentricity caused him to be regarded with some irritation, even derision, by some members of his community. His heart was so capacious that he had room in it not only for people of various denominations but also for those involved in approaches to healing other than medical and ecclesiastical orthodoxy. These included many psychic individuals who frequented spiritualistic societies because their gifts could not be accommodated within the ambience of the Church. Having been turned out of a living, albeit barely alive, tradition of true spirituality, they sought refuge among those who welcomed them from the realm of the occult. But this saintly monk could rejoice in their company and learn from them even as Jesus learned from the mass of humanity that he encountered and served day by day. The way of the heart is the culmination of humility, for it can imbibe knowledge from the lowliest of those its master meets in his unprentious work. Those who were befriended by this man were able to remain in the Church and not jettison everything on the waves of psychic phenomena.

A third person who works from the heart and who it is my privilege to know is a Benedictine monk who has an ashram in India and has played a notable part in bringing the deeper spirituality of Hinduism into harmony with the Catholic faith. The West needs desperately to understand aspects of the human spiritual anatomy and physiology that are an integral part of the Eastern tradition. This is not syncretism; it is a broadening of basic knowledge about the human condition, comparable in its way to an understanding of alternative therapies to complement the deficiences of orthodox allo-pathic medicine. This man has been able to accommodate Hindu insights in the context of the Christian faith, not primarily by his intellectual gifts but by his all-embracing love which allows people to be themselves without in any way trying to influence them according to a preconceived plan. In such a welcoming presence the person can be authentically himself without any pressure to conform, but the presence of the spiritual master leads the seeker onwards to the actualization of his full potential. This was the way of Christ among the common people: acceptance, spiritual transformation effected by his very presence, and the intuitive groping towards a new life. The only influence that may have a lasting effect on our fellows is a love that comes from the heart and opens the person to the full impact of the Holy Spirit.

The way of reconciliation has soon to confront the presence of darkness, the force of evil, in the world, and this is where it may appear to be inadequate. To assimilate it unconsciously is as dangerous as ingesting a poisonous substance in one's food. Our goodwill can no more detoxify a poison then neutralize evil, destructive forces in the world, forces which, if given free rein, would lead to a total dissolution of all civilized values and bring impenetrable darkness upon the world. On the other hand, the evil of the world which finds its reflection in the shadow side of our own personality, cannot be summarily excluded from our gaze, let alone outlawed from our inner life. Reconciliation may tend to underestimate the destructive element in life – which also finds its expression in the cruel perversions of all the higher religions – and in this respect its advocates, despite their openness of heart, may inadvertently allow the entry into the world of much that would have better remained excluded. But, on the other hand, the way of the heart is finally the only direction we know that can lead to universal healing. The wise man fears the spirit of evil but is not overwhelmed by its threat. Christ has shown us the way forward: submission to God in prayer, naked confrontation even to the extent of self-sacrifice, supernatural faith that comes from God even in the extremity of our own darkness, and a releasing of all worldly ties. The end is death of one type or another, but the sequel is resurrection.

Commitment strengthens our personal witness in the world in the face of all subversion and distraction. It develops the will and strengthens our spiritual potential. It leads to an uprightness that can easily proceed to a rigidity which precludes any spontaneous response to a matter of emergency. It can produce a determined, humourless type of person who does good in the world and practises virtue in his private life without any love of his neighbour; his actions are determined by an obsessive obedience to a higher power identified as God, but who instils fear without inculcating love. Such are the attributes of the great persecutors when they are not balanced by the flexibility that comes with tolerance. But without these firm attributes nothing positive can be done in the world, let alone the dimensions of the spirit. This follows the establishment of the centre within, where Christ has his eternal abode.

Once, however, commitment is fertilized by the spirit of love, our fear fades as we are able to contain conflicting ideologies no less than rebellious people in our hearts. The most inveterate conflicts arise from the contents of our own unconscious, which in turn are magnified by the dark forces that so often seem to be in control of the universe. But once the darkness within us is accepted, even welcomed, the way to reconciliation and healing becomes established. Christ then reigns in the soul; he transfigures all that we may encounter in our daily work. In this way the divine presence in the soul leads us patiently onwards towards the future advent of Christ in the world.

7

The Marks of Christ
(3) Peace and Awareness

Peace is commonly envisaged as a state of relaxation that follows the cessation of a period of strain. As the strain is eased, so does its legacy of stress on the afflicted person remit. Stress has deleterious effects on the body and mind. The muscles retain some degree of tension even while they are not in use, the digestion is impaired, the heart rate is accelerated, and the body's defences against assault are put on their guard even when there is no immediate threat. As a result of all those reactions, there is a dissipation of vital energy and the organs may in due course undergo organic changes that culminate in a number of common diseases such as raised blood pressure, stomach ulcers and possibly, even, some types of cancer. To be sure, none of these diseases has a single cause as yet known, arising rather from a number of circumstances acting together, but it does seem that the stressed individual is more at risk than his fellow who is relaxed and at peace in himself.

Associated with these physical phenomena there is a deeper unease: the mind cannot remain still, but is agitated and in a state of constant oscillation. It seems to be dominated by doubt and destructive thoughts. The emotional life registers fear, anxiety, suspicion and animosity. Even though there may be a semblance of silence, the mind continues in its onward race as if pursued by phantoms, the dark shadows of past regrets and future forebodings. It becomes jangled as it is caught in a vortex of inarticulate dissatisfaction, anger and dread.

In a silent retreat these menacing, destructive attitudes of mind, usually hidden beneath the plausible bonhomie of daily life, float up into consciousness. The censor of polite conversation is relaxed, and we are shown what proceeds in the depths, how dark influences of strife and betrayal muddy the still waters of the soul and lead to a general contamination of the personality. When we practise the silence that goes with a cessation of conversation, there is little to interrupt this exposure of our unconscious motives, so that great insight may be afforded into what our disposition is bestowing on the outer world which has to bear our constant discontent. The confrontation of this inner focus of subversion is aided by the still, compassionate acceptance that is such an important part of the general atmosphere of a retreat. Eventually the disorder within can be accepted, albeit with pain, and progressively assimilated into our conscious life. Then we at once know a freedom that was previously beyond our grasp and a fresh appreciation of the world around us slowly dawns. As the murky contents of the unconscious are allowed to rise gently to the surface, so the soul is cleared of much emotionally-charged debris. Then the inner Christ is allowed to act unimpeded, and we can obey Jesus' injunction. 'And you, like the lamp, must shed light among your fellows, so that, when they see the good you do, they may give praise to your Father in heaven' (Matthew 5:16). Then alone do we glimpse a peace that passes rational understanding, for it depends on our state of consciousness alone, and is not influenced by any worldly circumstance.

When the Christ within acts without the disturbance wrought by other, more superficial elements of the personality – whether unconscious or conscious – a glow permeates the individual which emanates as a radiance from him. This radiance is the essence of the power of the Holy Spirit that shows itself as a gift of healing. One can give healing to others only when one is open to God and to their need, an application of the two great commandments that underlie all spiritual activity. But for this complete openness to take place, we have first to be cleansed of concern, remembering that if we seek our comfort in a life of egoistical aloofness we court death, whereas a life that surrenders itself without demur to God and his gospel among the created whole, moves beyond death to a knowledge of eternal life. This self-surrender is, of course, a relinquishing of the ego that demands recognition and rewards. Once that ego becomes conversant with the law of service even to its eventual death, it reflects back to the source that gave it existence, the soul that in turn is sustained by God's Spirit. This soul by virtue of the divine presence directly within it, is immortal; once we begin to glimpse the promise of continuing life, we strain less obsessively at the glitter of this mortal life. This, incidentally, does not imply an indifference to personal well-being and bodily health without which earthly existence would be impossible, but a basic simplicity of our way of life so that we are less encumbered with possessions than previously and can proceed with the all-important work of service and reconciliation. It is in this frame of reference that we can most usefully consider Jesus' dictum about the impossibility of a rich man entering the heavenly estate.

When we are acquainted with the Christ within, we know of riches beyond measure; we no longer are driven to seek the world's wealth. The least of this wealth is material possessions – even a superficial glimpse can penetrate their imposing façade to the decay that eats away at their heart. Much more subversive are the good opinions of other people, so that we feel obliged to live up to their expectations – or what we believe are their expectations. In fact, however, most of us are absorbed in our own small domains and essentially negligent, if not predatory, in our relationships, at least until a deeper core of reality has been exposed in the course of our lives. No wonder that Jesus warned his disciples to tread warily when the masses spoke well of them, for thus had their predecessors addressed the false prophets; the speaker of truth seldom amasses plaudits for himself. This is because the false prophet flatters his disciples, and by his tidings of assurance exacts their support. The true prophet, on the other hand, brings divine judgement with him. Though he may, like Jeremiah, long for a life of inconspicuous comfort and quiet happiness even among the throng of evil doers, he cannot turn his back on the power of the Holy Spirit that impels him onwards to the pinnacles of truth, so soon to be confirmed by the march of events.

And yet, paradoxically, the tumult of abuse that surrounds the true prophet is closer to divine peace than the ferocious malice of those seeking to discredit him. For at the heart of the prophet there is God's presence fully active and guiding events in a way that transcends the understanding of all, even the prophet himself. At the heart of the populace the evil one stands in charge; he is at the helm of their affairs and his way veers inexorably towards destruction. Peace does not bring us quietness so much as intimate communion with God and with life as a whole. We may trust that even our contemporaries, despite their present hostility, will be led by the Holy Spirit in due course. This Spirit directs the mind into the way of critical self-knowledge, whose end is enlightenment and repentance that proceeds to an amendment of one's lifestyle. One can know peace in the depths of a man-made prison or in a hopelessly crippled body. There is often a radiant placidity around the blind who have accepted their limitation with gracious love, learning to regard it as a way to fulfil themselves in deep relationships with those around them. Indeed, when we have to retire from wage-earning activity, we should approach a state of peace in which we can start to confront our past life with mature understanding. As we come to terms with the fleeting figures of our active years in warm appreciation and open forgiveness, so we can await the future with the combined hope and awe that characterize a wise person. It also points to our attitude as we await Christ's full coming in glory among us at the end of our present dispensation. The peace of God is of a different order to a state of careless apathy tending to dull torpor in that it plays its part in the affairs of the world. It is concerned in the lives of the people in its vicinity. In one who lies imprisoned, whether in a dungeon or a decrepit body, the concern would be evinced in intercessory prayer for the world and deep caring for those in the person's immediate neighbourhood.

In all these instances the eclipse of executive activity together with the fading of the esteem and power one used to have in the world of affairs leads to the radiance of the soul being less obscured by worldliness and self-seeking attitudes. As the powerful created light of the sun fades, so does the inextinguishable uncreated light of the spirit shine forth with a welcoming radiance, even if it appears to be dulled during periods of depression and misfortune. Christ assumes his full stature in a soul that is cleared of the undergrowth of worldly ambition. When his presence assumes the majesty of the tree of life, his influence emanates from the person who now becomes a peacemaker, a very child of God's purpose. In the peace of God which the souls of the righteous enjoy in the life beyond death, there is an openness to the divine reality which we, working in the limitations of a physical body, can at most experience at infrequent intervals. The divine presence is unchanging, but so often do we erect almost impenetrable barriers of selfishness that prevent its entry into our lives; once these barriers are taken down, the presence is in our midst and we can enjoy all good things that flow from the Holy Spirit. This is peace, and it requires no straining on our part, only attention, acceptance and magnanimity for the sake of other people, who may be enabled to enjoy the holy fellowship with us.

It might be expected that peace of this intensity would so engage the full attention of the disciple that he would be dissociated from merely mundane affairs. Who would care to dine among humans after having attended the divine banquet! And yet the peace of God, like all other holy gifts, does not estrange us from our calling in life, raising us to a rarefied pinnacle of bliss in the clouds. On the contrary, it earths us more definitively than ever before so that we can devote our energies to the immediate task with renewed vigour and dedicated will. The Word himself became flesh and dwelt among us, during which time he experienced the full glory of the world and betrayal by those whom he loved. In the end his perfect life and the resurrection that followed his tortured death were to be the presage of the raising to eternal life of the whole cosmos. It therefore follows that the peace of God is an atmosphere of ceaseless activity for the sake of the whole created universe, an activity that is balanced, joyful and in perfect relationship with those around us. While an individual may lead in a special enterprise, no one is the master, for all are servants of God. It is, in fact, the body of Christ, a body of servants that transforms an indifferent world into a realm of vibrant, purposeful activity which ends in a transfigured universe.

The world of peace is the milieu of eternity, while the point of awareness is its focus in the present moment. Awareness in peace is the point where time intersects with eternity; it embraces the constant process of renewal by which the old and established are transfigured into a new order of creation. If our minds were quiet, ordered and focused on the present moment, we would be available to elevate that moment into a world of eternal glory. When the attention of Peter, James and John was completely focused on the transfigured presence of Christ, they were brought to a heightened awareness of the past as a prelude of the resurrection to occur in the future. Moses and Elijah, the final representatives of the Law and the prophets, had witnessed in their spiritual bodies the transfiguration as they contemplated the resurrection that was to complete the process of Jesus' life in the world and establish the pattern of his eternal presence among us.

That mind is most aware which is untroubled and at peace. A mind that wanders distractedly through a miasma of fears, regrets, anger and resentment, that loiters at the foothills of lust and avarice and paces around eddies of gossip and scandal can have no place in its meanderings for the present moment. In its feverish agitation it misses the present dispensation, it fails to recognize the divine providence at hand. And so it misses Christ in the context of the common experience that embraces all of us. Only when Christ comes in glory in the centre of our consciousness, in the soul's ground, do we begin to discern his traces in the world around us. The prerequisite of awareness is a quiet, active mind; if it is passive it is liable to invasion by complexes in the personal unconscious and psychic elements in the collective unconscious. Peace is far from a state of suspended animation in which we are open to any outside influence without discrimination. It is, on the contrary, a state of heightened awareness in which there is a needle-sharp application of the whole conscious apparatus to the minute at hand. We cannot attain that one-pointed awareness until our inner conflicts are acknowledged and are approaching resolution; then alone can we give ourselves totally to the present moment, no matter what it brings with it. As Jesus teaches, 'Each day has troubles enough of its own' (Matthew 6:34), but provided we set our mind primarily on God's Kingdom and his justice, all the rest of our requirements will come to us as well. Peace in Christ is the prescription for a way of life that allows us to be fully involved in the world at the present moment without in any way being submerged in it.

The end of spiritual awareness is to bring peace to everyone in our vicinity, to the world and finally to the entire created order. When we are at peace, the Kingdom of God is not merely within our grasp but is a part of our immediate consciousness. In that state we bring the Kingdom, or at least a knowledge of its presence, to all those whom we encounter in a day's work. This knowledge shows itself in a re-creation of the common order of life to the spiritual order that characterizes eternity. Its effect is one of realignment: when God created order out of chaos, life out of inanimate darkness, all that he made was good. Indeed, God's creation, by its very origin, mirrors its Creator. When the sentient, rational creature who had been endowed with the godlike quality of independent action, of free will, took control, he disturbed that natural order, that inherent goodness. From the energy of the Holy Spirit that gives life and purpose to all the creation, disturbed currents arose that put life out of alignment, that disrupted the onward flow of creation so that it turned against itself. Its constituent elements, its finite creatures, broke loose from the corporate union in which they had previously rested in God, albeit without awareness. Then they laboured for an ideal of egoistical supremacy; in so doing they fell into individualistic isolation, into separative existence, each in conflict with the other. They laboured under the illusory ideal of personal mastery, thereby sacrificing the communal goodwill on which all life depends. The genesis of evil lies in the assertiveness of individual consciousness which has broken loose from the corporate whole, whose fullness is God. As Jesus says, 'I am the real vine, and my Father is the gardener. Every barren branch of mine he cuts away; and every fruiting branch he cleans, to make it more fruitful still

66

. . . I am the vine, and you the branches. He who dwells in me, as I dwell in him, bears much fruit; for apart from me you can do nothing' (John 15:1–5).

The totality is Christ, who is also the central focus of the individual soul. When the individual breaks away from the totality, the energy that sustains him, the power of the Holy Spirit who is the lord of life and its giver, acts divisively against the whole. Though of divine origin, it now becomes a vortex of destructive activity, so being available for enormous mischief. The individual sets himself against Christ, known both as the peak of conscience and the universal whole in whom resurrection of the created order can alone take place. Only when there is a realignment of the natural order, so that the power of the Holy Spirit can be expended on a coherent scheme of life and growth, can peace be restored. This is the eternal way of spiritual progress, and in one form or another it characterizes the life of each person in the world, and no doubt in the spheres beyond our mortal experience. When the peace of God rules the soul of any one of us, the Spirit of God radiates from us and sets in harmony the disturbed emotions and perverse wills of those close to us. By the power of intercessory prayer that Spirit flows out in a milieu beyond time and space to all those who are open to our concern, effecting in them likewise a redirection of disordered emotional responses and a renewal of spiritual purpose.

It was indeed rightly said (by John P. Curran) that the condition upon which God has given liberty to man is eternal vigilance. If this is true in terms of national and international politics, it is even more fundamentally the case in regard to the peace of God that passes human understanding. Awareness is the greatest gift of peace as it is also necessary for the maintenance of that peace. When our minds are divested of disturbing passions, they can be fully about God's business, even as Jesus was as a boy of twelve in the temple at Jerusalem. We are fully free when we are about the divine work, for then we are raised in stature to Christ himself, doing our apportioned task in the fullness of our unique identity while strengthened by the power of Christ, who now directs proceedings unequivocally from the soul's centre. When, to quote St Paul, the life we live is no longer merely our own life but the life that Christ lives in us (Galatians 2:20), we attain the freedom to work at the height of our powers, at the zenith of our creativity, at the acme of awareness of the divine presence. To be constantly about God's business is to be at peace with the world, no matter how disturbed it may be. Only then can one be truly oneself and acutely aware of the passing moment.

When we are at peace within ourselves we can be aware of another person's plight. In the Parable of the Good Samaritan the priest and the Levite who passed by the man who had been assaulted and robbed were, in all probability, so preoccupied with their own business, so lost in their tortuous thoughts, that they were unaware and consequently unavailable to the demands of the greater world around them. There is a self-centredness based on unease and uncertainty within us that renders us oblivious of the needs of other people. The more we try to impress others, the more we betray our inner impotence. We are, in fact, in such a situation coveting the support of other people without in turn giving anything of ourselves to them. We attain that full awareness of unique identity when Christ within has integrated the elements of the personality so that we function as a complete whole. Then we have lost concern for ourselves and can flow out as an integrated person to anyone who needs our assistance. Our personality becomes the door to the vibrant inner life of the universe and also the portal to the needs of the world around us.

'Peace is my parting gift to you, my own peace, such as the world cannot give. Set your troubled hearts at rest, and banish your fears' (John 14:27). The things of this world cannot give us peace; the more we possess, the more attention is needed to protect them from the inroads of decay and the covetousness of those around us. The attributes of the personality, our gifts and attainments, on their own serve to separate us from others. We protect them against the threat of eclipse by those more proficient than ourselves, while they render us increasingly vulnerable by virtue of the jealousy they so easily foment. The presence of Christ within alone can bring our possessions and gifts into their right perspective:

they cease to be a means of self-assertion and become instead a blessing to the whole world. 'Full authority in heaven and on earth has been committed to me. Go forth therefore and make all nations my disciples' (Matthew 28:19). People are made disciples of Christ when he is allowed to reign as undisputed master in their souls. Only then do they respond to his call and enter fully into the corporate unity of his presence, the true body of Christ. Only then can the universal Church established in his name perform its lifegiving work of leading all people into the knowledge of his presence, into mutual fellowship, and into service for the entire created order. For we enter into complete fellowship one with another only when we are so free of self-concern that we can give of ourselves without reserve to the world and can, in return, receive the world into ourselves. In this act of pure exchange the Word within, the inner Christ, transforms the personality of us all from mere mortal dross to eternal radiance. The least of our fellows is seen to embody the Word by whom all things are made.

Peace is a state of being ourselves in whatever situation we may find ourselves. We can be authentically ourselves only when we function at the peak of our ability, a peak indicated by the action of Christ within us. When Christ is known in our present situation we pass beyond possessions to dominion. Then we are one with God to the extent that our mortal condition allows it – and, with the incarnate Lord, can give of ourselves to anyone we may meet on the road of life. The more we give, the more we receive of God's greatest gift, the Holy Spirit, which in turn flows out from us to all the world.

To be constantly aware, we must be at peace within ourselves and ardently concerned for the world outside. When our deepest desire is to give that peace to those around us, as Christ did in the final period of his ministry among his disciples, we have passed from solitary, individualistic isolation to an identification with all life. Then we do indeed become an instrument of God's peace. Just as Jesus brought order into the chaotic lives of those who were open to his ministry, so we too bring an inner calmness and resolution to all whom we serve. The secret of a truly living relationship between two people is a mutual self-giving that looks for nothing in return. And this indifference to personal satisfaction can be attained only when Christ rules over the heart and mind. With that presence in our midst all other favours and rewards are irrelevant, indeed they become increasingly deleterious to our well-being. Christ in us is our hope of a glory to come (Colossians 1:27). And when he is authentically the director of the soul, he takes his place among us also, directing all those in our vicinity into the way of peace and awareness. He, who is the undisputed master, is also the lowliest servant of us all. 'Another time, the tax-gatherers and other bad characters were all crowding in to listen to him; and the Pharisees and the doctors of the law began grumbling among themselves: "This fellow", they said, "welcomes sinners and eats with them" ' (Luke 15:1–2). But whoever dined with Jesus had his first experience of the heavenly banquet prepared for us all at the end of time.

8

The Four Last Things
(1) Death and Judgement

The end of mortal life is its distillation into an essence of lasting value, a product of significance that epitomizes the permanent value of the years spent on earth. The power that gives life is also the one that begins the process of our death. Death is to be seen not so much as a finite event in which we suddenly and inexorably give up the life of the body, as one in which the slow process of maturation and fruition culminates in the presentation of the personality to our Creator as a work finally consummated. The last words of Christ on the cross are traditionally cited as 'Father, into thy hands I commit my spirit' (Luke 23:46, quoted in turn from Psalm 31:5). We erect the spiritual body that will serve us in the intermediary realms of the afterlife while we are engaged in mundane activity: its bricks and mortar consist of our deeds, thoughts and attitudes as we go unobtrusively about our daily business. If we have no spiritual reserves, there will be little in the way of a spiritual body to accompany us in the world beyond death. These resources are the capital we have expended in service to our fellow creatures, who in turn will be there to greet us when we make the great transition.

It is a truth held in common by the spiritually aware of all the great religious traditions that we should remember God especially as we prepare to make the journey to the afterlife. If, however, we pay scant attention to the things of the spirit while all is going well with us, we will be in no frame of mind to call on the divine name when we are in a situation of extremity. On the contrary, the shock of our sudden danger and the terror of the unknown fate ahead of us are more likely to precipitate within us a state of helpless confusion and distraught fear. It is in this context that the story of Joseph and Pharaoh has its most universal significance: we, like the Egyptians, must conserve our stocks of produce during the years of prosperity, by the assiduous practice of prayer and good works, so that when the time of hardship befalls us, we may be able to fall back on our accumulated spiritual reserves. It is decidedly late in the day to think about God for the first time only when death approaches; fortunately, even then, there is hope for us provided we are truly penitent and sincere in our quest for truth.

The centre of our identity is the soul. It is God's gift to us, and his presence is immanent in the spirit. While the soul is in one respect merely the product of the life of a newly conceived embryo, it also seems to have an eternal life in the mind of God. Jeremiah was told that God knew him before he was formed in his mother's womb (Jeremiah 1:5). God knew him for his own, and he was consecrated before his birth, appointed to be a prophet to the nations. And so it may well be that our essence has an immortal quality, existing in God from the beginning of creation to the ultimate consummation of all things in Christ at the time of his final coming among us. The centre of the soul, the spirit, where God's presence lies, but so often ignored and disregarded, goes back to God at the time of our death. But what have we done with that spirit during our tenure of earthly life? This is, in effect, a variation on the theme of the formation of the spiritual body. We cannot know the answer to this sombre question while we are alive in the flesh. If we confidently believe we have enriched God's great gift to us during our period of incarnation, we may be sadly disillusioned when we approach the moment of judgement. How confidently did the Pharisee present himself in front of God in the temple, so sure that his piety had afforded him a place of honour in God's esteem and future favour! How aware, by contrast, was the publican of his own worthlessness! He seemed to have done nothing good with the spirit God had given him: his life appeared to be a total disaster.

And yet it was he, rather than the self-assured religious man, who was in right relationship with God, because he laid himself on the altar. In the words of Psalm 51, 'Thou hast no delight in sacrifice; if I brought thee an offering, thou wouldst not accept it. My sacrifice, O God, is a broken spirit; a wounded heart, O God, thou wilt not despise' (verses 16–17). As the rabbis taught, God wants the heart. This means the authentic soul-quality of the person illuminated with passion and consummated in love. The spirit that infused our earliest strivings during our time in our mother's womb is enriched by our experience in this fascinating mortal life that seems to be punctuated with so much hardship and anxiety. As we read in Psalm 90, 'All our days go by under the shadow of thy wrath; our years die away like a murmur. Seventy years is the span of our life, eighty if our strength holds; the hurrying years are labour and sorrow, so quickly they pass and are forgotten' (verses 9–10). The wrath of God of which the Psalmist speaks is the law by which all things are made, sustained and destroyed. It is wrath only if it is resisted selfishly, but if it is accepted it becomes the way of growth of the soul into the knowledge of eternity. 'The law of the Lord is perfect and revives the soul. The Lord's instruction never fails, and makes the simple wise' (Psalm 19:7). When we have come through the hard probationary period of suffering and diminishment, we will find ourselves at the heavenly footstool, accepted and renewed beyond all our wildest hopes. 'Well done, my good and trusty servant! You have proved trustworthy in a small way; I will now put you in charge of something big', as we read in the Parable of the Talents (Matthew 25:14–30).

The spirit that Jesus gave back to his Father as he expired on the cross had achieved mighty works of teaching and healing while it was incarnate: water had been turned into wine, and enormous miracles of supply had been performed. And yet it was by no means certain that Jesus had succeeded in what he had come to earth to achieve. His mission seemed to have ended on a note of dismal failure: once more the forces of evil appeared to have triumphed. I do not believe that the crucified Lord had any conception of the glory ahead of him. But God the Father received his spirit that had been immeasurably enriched by his life and ministry among men. The resurrection was the direct sequel to this mighty death in agony and uncertainty. Love is its own fruit; it looks for nothing outside itself, giving of itself without reserve even to death for its friend, who, in the context of Christ, is everyman. As St Paul puts it, 'On the human level he was born of David's stock, but on the level of the Spirit – the Holy Spirit – he was declared Son of God by a mighty act in that he rose from the dead' (Romans 1:3–4). The miracle of the resurrection, conveyed so wonderfully in the Gospels by the incredulous joy of the disciples, seems to be echoed by Jesus' own breathless delight as he shows himself to them. It was all so very unpremeditated, and this despite Jesus' prior teaching about the necessity of his death among sinners as the precursor to his rising to renewed life on the third day. The spirit he committed into the hands of his Father has indeed been enriched beyond all measure, and it was able to effect a complete bodily resurrection of a type outside the bounds of human comprehension, but nevertheless an earnest of the total resurrection of matter at the end of time.

When we die, we likewise will have to render to God an account of our spiritual journey on earth. If we approach the divine presence boasting of the wealth we had gained or the personal success we had achieved in our particular work or profession, we will find ourselves very poorly received. Nor can the dropping of important names or the citation of works of learning that we have left behind help us appreciably in the piercing scrutiny ahead of us. None of these things is in itself without value in our personal and spiritual growth so long as we enrich whatever we possess and whomsoever we encounter while we are functioning on earth. But as a means of self-identification, let alone self-commendation, they are objects of illusion; they will have dropped away from us even before the moment of transition. What alone remains with us at that critical time is the identity of the soul together with all it has learned emotionally and intellectually during its period of experience in the physical body. Its measure of attainment is its area of self-giving, and to its amazed delight it will find itself the centre of a vast concourse of friends in the greater life beyond death. Some of these it will have known in earthly life, but many more will be the members of the communion of saints unknown to it on a purely personal level. Indeed, the words of the Magnificat will ring especially true then: 'The arrogant of heart and mind he has put to rout, he has brought down monarchs from their thrones, but the humble have been lifted high. The hungry he has satisfied with good things, the rich sent empty away' (Luke 1:51–53).

As we have sown love in our personal relationships on earth, so will we be greeted with love by a vast multitude in the world beyond death. The reverse also holds true: the selfish, predatory type of person will have few to meet him, indeed he may be quite alone. This will be his judgement and his introduction to hell. In the somewhat enigmatic parable of the unjust steward, Jesus advises us to use our worldly wealth to win friends for ourselves, so that when money is a thing of the past we may be received into an eternal home (Luke 16:9). This appears to mean that it is our place to involve ourselves in the full workings of the world, sordid as it so frequently is, and to make relationships with a vast range of people, as Jesus did in his work among sinners whom the devout of his time would not touch, let alone befriend. When we die, any veneer of propriety we may disport, including our association with vogue trends in world affairs will be an episode behind us, a thing of the past. We will be judged by what we are in ourselves. God wants the heart: in the gathering dusk it is our charity that alone affords the light that guides us towards our place of reception. That light is also the measure of judgement ahead of us. It is only when Christ rules our hearts that we can become involved with all types of people, lifting them up to God as Jesus did in his work with those who were open to his love. That love emanates as a pure light that leads all those we once knew to the eternal life beyond death. Some may have indeed preceded us in the great journey ahead of us all, but our spiritual light will have guided them even in realms we yet have to traverse in our own experience.

The judgement ahead of us is presided over by God, but the jury comprises our fellow beings now inhabiting the realms of the afterlife. It is important to remember that eternity includes our life on earth no less than the life of the soul after physical death. We know eternity now if we lead an active spiritual life of prayer and worship amid our duties and calling, hour by hour. We are indeed preparing for the hour of our death while we are vigorously alive in the world by remembering God constantly in prayer and practising right relationships with all those in our vicinity; in the end these include the entire created order, since we are all parts of the one Body whose name is Christ. At the seat of judgement we will be aware of the person of Christ, perhaps for the first time. In his presence we will wilt before his holiness, even though his nature is one of unfailing forgiveness and healing. He will receive us with kindness, and then send us about our business firmly and decisively. But how will we recognize him, for he is no longer known as a discrete person? We will know him by the atmosphere of love, light and power that he emanates: his is absolute authority and grace. This atmosphere marks his presence, reminding us of the statement in John 4:24, 'God is spirit, and those who worship him must worship in spirit and in truth.'

Even when Jesus revealed himself at the period of the resurrection he was no longer recognizable as he had been before his death: he was seen as an anonymous gardener by Mary Magdalene, a fisherman by the apostles and a visionary stranger by those journeying to Emmaus. It was only by some word or gesture that he revealed himself incontestably to his disciples. Since the time of his ascension, he comes to all of us as a mystical presence when we are capable of receiving him. In this way we are preserved from the temptation of reducing him to a form that we can possess and control. Instead, he can raise us up above the limits of circumscribed personality to an identity that includes all people, indeed eventually the entire created order. He comes to us as an atmospheric presence to lift us out of our blind immersion in matter to a vision of the glory that transfigures all material substance into spiritual radiance. In this way we are freed, albeit for a short time only, from the shackles of mortality so that we may enter upon the liberty and splendour that is our destiny as children of God (to quote freely from Romans 8:21). As we attain this glory, so we bring the universe itself with us, until the time of the general resurrection when all matter is spiritualized, when all that exists returns to God, transfigured by the power of the Holy Spirit.

In this respect, how will we recognize our loved ones in the intermediate realms beyond death? There will be no physical body, and although it may be possible for the spiritual body we have fashioned during earthly life to condense sufficiently to assume an opacity that may delineate the contours of the form we once possessed, this appearance, or apparition, will not indicate our real identity. It is to be seen rather as a consolation to the bereaved who are psychically sensitive; in it they may be assured of the continued presence of their loved one. But our true being is manifested in the soul presence that we continue to register after physical death. Indeed, it is the soul that is the seat of our true identity even while we are alive in the flesh; by contrast, the physical body undergoes a constant change. The bodily configuration of our youth bears scant likeness to our physical form in middle life and especially to the shrunken features of old age. But the soul that witnesses the changing scene of bodily growth and senescence remains intact. To be sure, it should grow in compassion and wisdom with the years of earthly experience behind it, but its unique flavour is not disguised, let alone annulled, at least if we are attempting to live an honourable life in relationship with God and our fellow creatures. When we die, this soul that animated the physical body when we were alive in the flesh is now completely bare. No longer can it remain hidden behind the coarse opacity of the body of flesh and bones we inhabit in this world. Instead, it shows itself naked and unadorned, and as such is recognized by all who knew it in its earthly limitation. As in the instance of Christ among us, whose presence is that of an incandescent radiance and a warm invitation to holiness, to dine with him as host at the heavenly banquet, so we ourselves also show our true nature by what we have established and attained spiritually during our life on earth. If we had the discernment to know a person in his full integrity, we would have the ability to glimpse the soul that revealed itself, however unobtrusively, in the course of his incarnate existence. This is the true knowledge of the self; it is incontrovertible, for it lies within and does not depend on the circumstances of the outside world.

It is no accident that people of sanctity are encompassed by an emanation of unearthly radiance which has been depicted unerringly by the great painters of the past who still had an inner eye for such details of spirituality; the inner vision was projected to an outer physical manifestation as the mind informed the visual apparatus of the brain and eye. This radiance is the undistorted light of the Holy Spirit that pours out from a soul that is empty of guile and therefore a pure chalice of divine grace. By contrast, unwholesome people with great charm and psychic presence can appear to be invested by a glitter that may serve to beguile and confuse those who are spiritually inexperienced and who judge by superficial appearances. Unlike the light of sanctity that seems to transfigure the whole person, the glitter that plays on the less worthy person is superficial and does not illuminate him so much as outline his character.

It would seem that this light also finds its origin in the Holy Spirit, from whom all light proceeds. He is defined credally as the lord and giver of life. But those whose wills are perverted, who have offered themselves, however unobtrusively, to the guidance of demonic forces, manipulate and deflect the power of the Holy Spirit. This power then becomes interior and a private force of self-assertiveness. It indeed enters into the life of the individual, becoming, with him, sequestered, increasingly isolated, and cut off from the full flow of life. It serves the personality of the one who misuses it, but as a consequence he becomes progressively separated from his neighbours. This is the way in which naked evil becomes established and flourishes in its destructive power. It is, however, slowly isolated from the world before its final, inevitable destruction. All this, dimly intelligible to those who are spiritually aware on this side of death, becomes increasingly clear to those no longer encumbered by a mortal body and existing as a delicate soul structure functioning in a spiritual body of varying completeness.

A soul of high stature is so transparent that the divine presence within it is fully apparent to the world: it is one with God. This state of affairs is fully applicable to Christ, but when we shed all mundane encumbrances even now and live in pure simplicity in the present moment, we too can start to become the agents, albeit unconscious of our role, of lifting up in a most amazing way all that lies around us to the very presence of God himself. This is in fact a most significant aspect of the judgement: do we remain in a state of darkness, such as characterizes the faces of so many of our compatriots, or is there the radiance of celestial light illuminating our inner being and shining from us to the world around us? This light is our lantern, guiding us to the place prepared ahead of us. At the same time it reveals our unique presence to the vast concourse of persons, saint and sinner alike, both with us in the flesh and in the greater world beyond death. The spiritual body that is being fashioned while we are alive on earth is composed of soul substance: the soul becomes increasingly diaphanous as the spiritual body increases in substance. The whole unit is infused by the Holy Spirit, and its content is progressively transfigured until it becomes an unobstructed channel for the light of God, a flawless instrument of God's grace.

By contrast, the spiritually debased person whose life has rotated around an axis of unashamed self-seeking, of heedless selfishness, is inwardly opaque. The black opacity renders him unresponsive and impenetrable to God's grace, because he has never sacrificed anything of himself to the world around him, indeed to any living form outside himself. It is in this frame of understanding that we can glimpse some deeper implications of the Parable of the Rich Man (Dives) and Lazarus (Luke 16:19–31). The man of wealth and heedless self-indulgence has a soul so dark that it cannot be illuminated by any spark of recognition, let alone compassion, for his fellow creatures. It is therefore also beyond the possibility of infusion by the light of God. This is the nature of the gulf that separates him from the beggar, now lying in rest in heaven. The darkness of soul cannot be expunged simply by a cry for help, or even a sincere regret for the past and a desire to save his brothers from a similar fate. Like the nine lepers who, having been healed by Jesus, did not so much as turn back and give thanks to God for their marvellous recovery (Luke 17:11–19), it is all too probable that the rich man in hell would equally rapidly have dismissed from his memory his present circumstances, had they been summarily reversed. For him to become converted sincerely to God and effect an amendment of life, some greater commitment than mere remorse would be necessary before there would be any chance of his tasting the divine mercy. To know the mercy of God which sustains us each day requires of us in turn a self-giving approach to life. This self-giving is an attitude of blessing to all around us, made tangible by acts of love. This attitude, on the one hand, is our response to God's unfailing love towards us – we love because he loved us first – but it requires of us an attention to God so absolute that we have left our own desires behind us. Once in this manner we are open to God for himself alone, without the dark diversion of subversive thoughts of personal advantage, we are in a state to receive the divine grace. This self-yielding, which is the key to openness, will eventually attain that perfect knowledge of love in which we are prepared to give up our life for our friend – who, in the reality of God, is everyman.

Applying this sequence to the rich man in hell, in Jesus' parable, he would have to face the necessity of a total sacrifice of himself, with the possibility of total extinction, before there could be an authentic cleansing of his soul from darkness. Only when, like Abraham who was ready to give up Isaac to God, the rich man showed himself prepared for the ultimate sacrifice, would the miracle of God's grace have descended upon him. His life would have been renewed, the gulf bridged so that the Holy Spirit could work freely in him, and a disposition to holiness established that would have influenced many others besides the rich man himself. The immutable law of cause and effect which mirrors God's constant vigilance and justice cannot be set aside to suit our convenience. But if, in the suffering that our evil actions have brought down upon us, we can withstand all overt rebuffs to our constant pleas for mercy and persist in an attitude of humble penitence, the time will come when our souls will have opened sufficiently to receive God's love. That divine love never fails, but we have to be ready to receive it. When we do receive it in the depths of our being, we are changed as people, and at last start to do the work ahead of us from our present vantage point. This becomes our place of destiny from which we move in the direction of our final destination.

The judgement of God which is enacted in the attitudes of those around us in the dimension of the afterlife is final, but the consequences of that judgement, the punishment that derives from it, have a dynamic thrust. They tend towards our healing, they redeem us from the bondage of past wrongful attitudes and tend towards our reinstatement in the larger existence ahead of us. What is needed of us in an unstinting dedication to the world in which we now function. The punishment is not unending unless we choose to make it so, but the responsibility for our inadequate past life cannot be evaded or shifted on to those around us. The way towards amendment of life starts with an unclouded awareness of the part we have played in our own failure to live up to the high mark set before us by Christ within us. In this frame of mind the very idea of passing the blame on to the circumstances of our birth, upbringing or employment appears increasingly irrelevant, at least in an afterlife situation. We see more clearly that we are expected to grow spiritually through our misfortunes and trials. They are not here simply to be used as an excuse for antisocial behaviour and a generally wasted span of life on earth. Job's misfortunes, manfully if rebelliously borne, brought him closer to God than did all his previous devotions designed quite deliberately to appease God's wrath and curry his favour.

It is an arresting paradox that the more we take refuge in excuses, the further away do we move from our fundamental integrity. It is far more praiseworthy to confront our weakness directly, even triumphantly. Jacob, not a particularly saintly man, stood his ground when he was attacked by a heavenly presence: Jacob would not let him go until he had obtained a blessing from him. As a result he attained a heightened spirituality symbolized in his change of name to Israel: one who has shown strength with God and is subsequently to be a champion of God. Thus Jacob transcends his previous self-centredness, and assumes the stature of a patriarch. In a somewhat different context Job, too, stood up for his integrity; in fact he had little to repent of in the vision of the soul. And in the end he gained the unexpected reward of seeing God in as close an intimacy as is permitted mortal flesh.

As we are able to accept suffering and integrate its fruits

into our lives, without resentment on the one hand or evasion on the other, so we prove ourselves adequate for the great work lying ahead of us. Our very failings can make us lovable when they are faced with courage and given to God on the altar as a sacrifice. The afterlife scene, far from being a place of finality and rest, is one of unceasing activity for the sake of the world and all that dwells in it.

9

The Four Last Things
(2) Hell

The essential feature of hell is isolation. This isolation separates us both from God and from our fellow creatures. And yet we remain aware of our own identity, which now takes on the terrifying character of a separated consciousness devoid of any communication outside itself. This is a state of hell. I am aware of myself and even more aware of my total separation from any being who cares about me. Thus I become a no-person, a thing of no finite existence, in a milieu that carries on its own business oblivious of me. I cease to exist in its calculations while I am acutely aware of my own existence, albeit in a total void. In the world of time and space that we inhabit in bodies of flesh and blood, the equivalent of hell is a state of being lost in a labyrinth of subterranean caverns, shouting frantically and hearing only the echoes of our own terror. There is no one else to register the sound or to be at all concerned that we are missing from our usual position in the world's economy. A terrible claustrophobia overwhelms us, and we can scarcely bear the impress of our consciousness while at the same time flinching in horror at the possibility of our total extinction. Furthermore, we begin to understand that we are responsible for this appalling state of affairs. Like the rich man Dives in hell, we grasp with horror how our heedless way of life has borne the fruits of total isolation, whether on earth or, even more terrifyingly, in the vast realms of post-mortem existence. Indeed, in the parable of Dives and Lazarus, the rich man at least enjoys some communication with Abraham and Lazarus even if an unbridgeable gulf separates them from direct contact. In the hell of common life there may be little effective communication with any sentient form, and the isolation appears to be absolute.

Hell and heaven are no strangers to our inner awareness: we harbour both in our soul. When the consciousness leading to hell dominates our thoughts and actions, we act autocratically and without consideration for the needs and feelings of those around us. We use them without giving of ourselves to them in concern. People who act in this self-centred way lack sensitivity; they are unaware of the feelings of those around them, and are indeed in a state of inner isolation even when they are dominating the local scene. As they are in hell, so they bring the knowledge of that hell to whomsoever they meet. In the end that hellish contamination can pervert the attitudes of a large number of morally ambiguous people who have neither awareness nor peace about them. They fall into the plausible and always attractive delusion that self-actualization is dependent upon wealth, power and worldly knowledge. When all these phantoms dissolve in the enormous finality of death, there is nothing left and the person collapses into a state of punctured emptiness. He is derelict with no one to acknowledge, let alone comfort him. His knowledge of God is likewise eclipsed, because his selfish career has acted as a shutter against the entry of the divine grace into his life. Just as the sun is obliterated from our sight by a heavy layer of cloud, so is the divine presence separated from us by our attitudes of self-sufficiency and arrogance. Both God and the great communion of saints are close to the person in hell, but they cannot make their presence felt. Individual free will is sacrosanct in the divine plan. Until we face our past selfishness and our betrayal of the lives of other people, commending ourselves in abject humility to God's grace, there is no remedy for this terrible experience of isolation. The psychical counterparts of this hellish realm are a thick darkness that obliterates any knowledge of divine love and purpose, and a sense of impending dissolution that brings with it a terrible awareness of meaninglessness and corruption, even to the point of ultimate chaos.

Hell is not extinction; God's nature, which is always one

of mercy, will not allow any creature to be destroyed. The position is put with searing poignancy by Hosea in respect of unfaithful, adulterous Israel; 'How can I give you up, Ephraim, how surrender you, Israel? . . . My heart is changed within me, my remorse kindles already. I will not let loose my fury, I will not turn round and destroy Ephraim; for I am God and not a man, the Holy One in your midst' (Hosea 11:8–9). But the fact of hell cannot be gainsaid, let alone conveniently put on one side for future consideration. God himself cannot alter the position of a person incarcerated in hell because his gift to us of free will is sacrosanct. He can stand in quiet patience at the door of the soul and knock, but he has denied himself the privilege of forcible entry. Love can never fail, but neither can it claim power over the beloved nor inflict itself upon him. St Paul saw quite plainly that love is never boastful, conceited or rude, but there is no limit to its faith, hope and endurance (1 Corinthians 13:4–7). Love is indeed the strongest of all powers, and in its capacity for total self-giving, the most terrible, for it comes from God and will not desist in its concern until the object of its ardour comes to himself, until the person unfolds into a radiant being of full humanity as measured in Christ himself. And yet the reception of God at the portal of self-awareness is a function that the soul alone can perform. To it belongs the power of welcoming God, of effecting an entry of the divine love into its own domain. The end of love is the liberation of the beloved from the prison of separateness, so that he attains divine knowledge, the very vision of God.

If severe punishment in hell is due to a self-centred way of life in the past, it is added to by the unremitting love of God. This love will never discharge the erring one from God's presence, even though he steadfastly refuses to acknowledge that presence, let alone open himself to the love, a love that flows eternally from the divine face in the person of the Holy Spirit. There is therefore a terrible impasse: the creature's recalcitrance contends with the divine compassion; while the former prevents an openness to participating in life, the latter prevents an extinction of the creature. Divine love grapples with human pride, and the confrontation may continue indefinitely. As in our world we cannot compel our compatriots to like us, so God too cannot wring obedience from a rebellious creature. But as in mundane life a special circumstance may spontaneously evoke sympathy and deep respect from our bitterest enemy, so it may be that in the end the man of pride may repent and become available to the experience of God's forgiveness that opens the way to the knowledge of love. Love acts on a cosmic plane in contrast to affection, which is more limited in its scope and variable in intensity. But the circumstance that may precipitate a change in heart in a man of pride has often to be a period of very severe suffering. This is an aspect of the mystery of hell and redemption. It is important to remember that our survival is an expression of God's love, not our own merit. Nevertheless, survival of death, though a blessing, has in addition the sombre consequence of forcing us to confront our own inner hell. Until this is fully inspected and explored, the work of the soul in the afterlife can scarcely commence. As the soul becomes increasingly transparent with the release of dark, unconscious material, so it becomes a more fitting chalice of God's indwelling light.

In such a scheme there is a gradual ascent of the soul from the dark isolation of hell to the more bearable planes of an intermediate state, traditionally called purgatory in Catholic theology. It is essentially a milieu of purification; the suffering here is one of increasing self-knowledge, so that the soul can see with devastating clarity the sins of omission it had committed during earthly life and also the considerable cruelty that had flowed from its distorted attitudes, a cruelty that had hurt, even maimed, the lives of many people whom the individual had encountered in social and personal relationships. The statement of Christ, 'There are many dwelling-places in my Father's house; if it were not so I should have told you; for I am going there on purpose to prepare a place for you' (John 14:2), suggests, as far as the intangible nature of ultimate reality can be gauged, that the discarnate soul has to undergo many experiences in its future existence. According to William Temple in his *Readings in St John's Gospel*, those dwelling-places, or mansions, are wayside caravanserais – shelters at stages along the road where travellers may rest on their journey. The basis of these experiences is varied relationships with other people, however we can envisage a person in this larger framework of vibrant life in spheres beyond our little world. In the end, soul growth shows itself in the two cardinal qualities of love and wisdom; both of these are gradually attained through the manifold experiences of life held in common with others of similar soul constitution. In other words, we grow in inner knowledge through our contact with other people, so that the less desirable aspects of psychic, or soul, life are gradually exposed, acknowledged, accepted and transfigured. These undesirable qualities are all centred around the desire for self-aggrandizement to the detriment of other people in our midst. The soul itself is an amphibious unit, having contact both with the divine and the demonic aspects of reality. This is typical psychic consciousness, essential in terms of meaningful communication with other people and with God, but also liable to be infiltrated and perverted by influences from the destructive layers of existence.

The psychic realm is that of direct soul communication from one individual to another. When the people heard Jesus, they were astounded by his teaching, for, unlike the doctors of the law, he taught with a note of authority (Mark 1:22). This authority issued from the depth of Jesus' being, his soul, and it evoked an immediate response in the souls of the masses who heard him. We may be sure it was not the intellectual sweep of his teaching that arrested them, for the common man is no theologian; it was rather the soul-quality of Christ that evoked the Spirit of God immanent in the souls of his eager audience, and all who were receptive were given their first taste of the Kingdom of God. In our smaller world, it is likewise the psychic outflow that determines the depth of a relationship between one person and another; intellectual agreement is a much more superficial factor, liable to wane as other matters supplant it in the lives of the people. The soul contact, by contrast, is much more durable. It seems probable, as far as we can conceive of such things, that the souls of the deceased effect a similar psychic communication with each other in the realms of the afterlife and, rather more evidentially, with the souls of those who are still alive in this world, according to the well-documented material of psychical research.

However, psychic communications can as easily be of evil import as of good. When a compelling demagogue addresses the masses, the burden of his message is usually one of hatred against a particular class or group in the society in which they live. If his outlook harmonizes with the prevailing ethos, the crowds can be led into terrible excesses against the objects of their fear and jealousy. The early career of Hitler, the supreme master of darkness in our century, is an eloquent example of evil communication transmitted psychically, but he is, in fact, merely a notorious example of a tendency well known among groups seeking power even to the extent of world domination. None of the major world religions has been innocent of this tendency in its darker periods. Just as the healing psychic communication of Jesus had its origin in God the Father – the Son can do nothing by himself; he does only what he sees the Father doing (John 5:19) – so the destructive psychic communication of a demagogue has its origin in the demonic influences among the hierarchy of angels. These can communicate their vindictive message, or attitude, to all who are psychically sensitive and at the same time harmonize inwardly with the evil material the demonic entities are transmitting. Those who are sympathetic to the message of hatred from the cosmic spheres provide an admirable repository for that hatred in the unconscious part of their own psyche. And so darkness infiltrates the soul, obfuscating the light of God within it to the point of threatening to destroy that light absolutely.

It is thus that we return once more to the Prologue to the Fourth Gospel: 'The light shines on in the dark, and the darkness has never mastered it.' Nevertheless, as we have observed previously, neither has the light ever mastered the darkness. The cosmic conflict continues unabated, and in our present dispensation, it appears to be mounting a breathless climax to the final field of decision. We in our world constitute a microcosm that mirrors, and at the same time influences, the macrocosm: the cosmic battle between the forces of light and darkness, of life and extinction. It is a bold thought that our minuscule human civilization can affect the cosmic flow as much as the cosmos exerts its influence in our world. Nevertheless, it is true: we are all so integrally part of the one

Body, whose extent is coincident with the created universe and whose Creator is God in his threefold capacity of Father, Son and Holy Spirit, that we exert a psychic influence on the furthest galaxy, indeed the furthermost conceivable astronomical universe, commensurate with the influence that the cosmos exerts on our small planet and indeed on our individual psychic awareness. The mystics have always known of the interconnectedness of all things: William Blake states this unforgettably in his *Auguries of Innocence*, 'To see a world in a grain of sand and a heaven in a wild flower, hold infinity in the palm of your hand, and eternity in an hour'. Indeed, in this passage, Blake explains the cosmic relationship that permeates all the creation: it is brought into one in the spiritual dimension that transcends all space and time, finding its being in God alone. In him we live and move, in him we have our being (Acts 17:28).

When we function from the depth of our being, when indeed we are in communion with our soul, we are in similar communion with all our fellow creatures. What we send out is our own essence, pure and simple, and without any intellectual or social accretion that might tend to obscure our true identity. In such fellowship we are a focus of healing to all those in our vicinity. When, however, we are not acting from the soul, there may be a less desirable psychic contact between us and those around us; this unconscious connection can drain us or them, or even both of us simultaneously if we are in contact with deep, dark areas of the unconscious that are more likely to be energized by the demonic strata of the psychic world than its beneficial angelic forces. In other words, when we live and work in awareness and control of ourselves, God is the master and what we give out is good, but when we are not functioning on the level of the soul we are in danger of being submerged by dark psychic currents proceeding from the unconscious which in turn is part of the collective unconscious wherein dwell the demonic as well as the angelic powers. Nevertheless it is the demonic that invariably prevails in a personality that has yielded its power of decision to forces external to itself. The crucial test is whether we call in reverence on the name of God, in whose name alone there is salvation (Joel 2:32, quoted in Romans 10:13). Usually God is absent from our thoughts.

Hell is a state of total psychic darkness in which the person can distinguish no outer form and yet is terrifyingly aware of his own presence to the void. This is the inner experience of hell: one that Jesus above all else accepted for the sake of the world. The greatest affliction, I believe, occurred in Gethsemane when he had to flounder in asphyxiating fumes of darkness, completely alone: his three disciples were nowhere available in terms of awareness, while God's presence was obliterated by the thickness of the stench of evil. This was Jesus' psychical separation from God and the world. In the agony on the cross the psychic barrier had, to some extent, been lifted, but in full view of the hostile crowd he had to show his naked impotence, not altogether dissimilar to that of a newborn infant. But whereas the infant may rely on the solicitude of those around it, Christ had to parry the darkness of human rejection and abuse. The darkness was now of a more rational quality: it seemed as if God's providence was an illusion, and that his own mission was a ghastly failure, indeed a fundamental error. We all, at one time or another, whether in this life or in the life beyond mortal death, have to undergo the experience of hell, not so much because of our deserts but for the sake of the invaluable experience it affords us of the nature of evil and the necessity of developing our spiritual faculties to deal with it and to help others who may later fall into the same darkness. Our health, whether physical or psychical, is of paramount importance, because without it we cannot serve our fellow creatures adequately. But even the experience of failing health, and the limitation it imposes on our powers to act and serve, can bring us to a completely different understanding of service in waiting and prayer. Those three women who stood mutely at the foot of the cross probably supported Jesus more effectively than anyone else as he gave up his spirit to God.

The essential difference between the type of hell suffered by a good man like Job, Jeremiah or especially Jesus, and that in store for those whose way of life is predatory and destructive of the happiness of others is that the good person's suffering, though terrible, is informed with a knowledge of

90

personal integrity. He does not lose contact with his deep centre, the soul with its indwelling spirit . . . 'all that came to be was alive with his life, and that life was the light of men' (John 1:4). Therefore there is an inextinguishable hope in the depth of his being that refuses to be suppressed despite the apparent hopelessness of his cause. By contrast, the hell ahead of the sensual hedonist who cares for no one except himself is an interminable darkness in which all the worldly landmarks are obliterated. He gropes in vain for a light to show him his position, but there is none to reveal his whereabouts, let alone direct him on the way. Since his concern was only for the things of the flesh, once these have dwindled there is nothing onto which he can cling, let alone aspire towards in the future that is a Stygian blackness before him. He may console himself by conjuring up images of the past to assuage his present dereliction, but these are more illusions; they have no substance in them. In a like manner, after the death of such a degraded individual, there will be no visible landmarks to a future state of being to guide him along the path. He may therefore remain earthbound to the extent of frequenting his former place of residence, oblivious of his present position among the ranks of the deceased, and therefore unaware that he has no further claims on the things of this world. Until he begins to understand his present position and call for help, he will remain fixed, a situation we have already discussed in detail in regard to the Parable of Dives and Lazarus. Those who are involved in the ministry of deliverance are called on from time to time to aid in the release of earthbound 'spirits', or entities. While some are extremely malicious, the majority are simply ignorant and unaware; when alive in the flesh they led selfish, heedless lives and are now reaping the fruits of their labours. They, like the inhabitants of Jonah's Nineveh, cannot tell their right hand from their left, and are indeed not much raised in moral consciousness above the cattle without number that accompany them. Yet God cares for them all and will rescue them, provided they, like the Ninevites, repent and purpose an amended life in the future.

The tragedy, and also the supreme glory, of the human condition, is that the spirit is willing but the flesh weak. If the spirit leads us to God, the naked flesh is more open to the wiles and enticements of the dark forces of the earth and the psychic realm. And yet the flesh is as necessary for the full flowering of the spirit as the spirit is for the full resurrection of the flesh. The conflict of the 'lower nature', as incarnated in the flesh, with the higher, spiritual nature that St Paul especially defines in Romans 8:1–13, is not ultimately won for God by the spiritual side triumphing to the detriment of the flesh. Indeed, the more we view with historical hindsight the great battles of mankind and their subsequent aftermath, the more do we realize that there are no final victors other than the power of unredeemed evil. The way of God is a total restoration of all things in their own integrity, for God has created all things in their own form. Even our weaknesses may play their part in the healing of the psychic darkness that so often appears to dominate the life of all the world's creatures. The meaning and fate of evil in the scheme of reality is the final mystery.

10

The Four Last Things
(3) Heaven

If hell is a state of isolation from all existence save oneself, heaven is the environment of complete intimacy with all creatures, so that nothing is hidden and all is shared. At the apex, or centre, of this divine community is the Spirit of God who infuses all things with his radiance, a radiance of light contained in a glow of warmth. And yet the Spirit cannot be localized to any one focus or area in this great concourse, which in any case is depicted only metaphorically in terms of space and time. Heaven is the realm of the Spirit, but so also is hell. As Psalm 139 puts it so clearly, 'Where can I escape from thy spirit? Where can I flee from thy presence? If I climb up to heaven, thou art there; if I make my bed in Sheol, again I find thee' (verses 7–8). The presence of God not only marks all dimensions of existence, it also determines their existence. 'No single thing was created without him' (John 1:3). The descent of Christ into hell, a descent effected from the moment of his baptism up to the time of his resurrection, signifies not only the divine dominion of that region but also the divine participation in its workings prior to its own redemption.

Nevertheless, the presence of God in heaven is manifest whereas in hell it is obscure, available only to those who seek with a diligence that follows profound suffering. Since God is the centre as well as the periphery of heaven, all arc open and available to him. Inasmuch as the deepest secrets are in the divine custody, nothing can be withheld from him. Since

93

his nature is always one of love with its corollary of forgiveness, there is no longer any inclination on our part to hide
anything from him, and therefore, secure in his love, we can
give of our inner life without reserve to those around us, at
the same time accepting their confidence with equal openness.
In the story of Adam and Eve, when they had excluded
themselves from a direct relationship with God, which is the
full measure of heaven in our life, they realized their nakedness and started to hide themselves. In time each person
became an enclosed unit intent on guarding his own interests
from the intrusion of all others except those close in regard
to himself; the family unit became in effect an extension of
individualism, and each family fought with its neighbour for
supremacy. With the advent of Christ in the soul, the seed of
God germinating to become a precious, tender shoot, love
began to supplant militant egoism and co-operation replaced
individualistic strife. Then at last mutual confidences could
be exchanged, and the mounting disorder in any soul divulged
and relieved. What we can start to discharge into the general
psychic atmosphere, provided love is in command of the
situation, will be redeemed, no matter how diseased it is. At
the same time we, relieved of the incubus of our mounting
internal disorder, know a peace of mind previously beyond
our imagination. The sudden void that appears is at once
filled with love, and we start to lead a new life of openness
to all creatures on the one hand and to God on the other.

One does not know heaven until one is well acquainted
with hell: the resurrection was the final sequence in a long
journey through hell in which Jesus showed himself the friend
of all who walk that path. This, of course, means everyman.
Only when the illusion of separation drops from us in the
course of our life on earth, do we move definitively from the
hell of self-inflicted isolation to the heaven of a self-giving
intimacy in which an increasing number of people find their
place. This does not mean that we will never know darkness
and isolation again, for our path is intimately related to that
of our brother with us on the way. But we will now share
that darkness with God, who will be a conscious presence
with us, so that we will not experience the dereliction of

purposelessness – meaningless confusion in the absence of all companionship.

It may be argued that complete intimacy is incompatible with the integrity of the individual; each person should have his own place of retreat, his own sanctum of privacy. This is undoubtedly true of our world, where to let in strangers without reserve would in effect be to destroy our own lives. Indeed, the more one advances along the spiritual path, the more essential does one find periods of stillness and times of withdrawal amid the psychic, no less than the physical, tumult of everyday life. Jesus himself escaped from the crowds whenever he could so that he might commune in silence (this is a fine definition of contemplation in all its nuances) with his Father in heaven. He strove to bring the disciples with him on many such occasions, so that they too could learn the art and practice of prayer. In those surroundings the disciples experienced an even deeper impression of heaven than they did when in Jesus' company in the marketplace. In one respect merely being in his company was heaven, because where he was, there was the Father also. But the disturbed, and therefore disturbing, emotional currents that played around them detracted from that heavenly peace, easily diverting the distractable minds of the disciples along other less profitable paths – the paths of self-interest at the expense of the greater community.

On the other hand, the purpose of shared silence and communal withdrawal, as on a conducted retreat, is to bring us back into the disturbed world more able to cope with its conflicts, more able to apply the balm of considered re-flection to a situation of raw malice. We can do none of this through our own good intentions; only God's grace working through us can achieve the rationally impossible. It is thus also that the complete intimacy of heaven in no way threatens the individual integrity of the soul. Because God is manifestly at the centre, all is transformed in his presence to the perfect replica of Christ as manifested in its own identity: 'The life I now live is not my life, but the life which Christ lives in me', is the way St Paul expresses this insight (Galatians 2:20). Christ does not take over our life so that we cease to be ourselves. What he does is to transform it so that at last we function as we were intended to do, as a child of God in our particular framework, which is obviously unique and therefore different from the framework of Jesus of Nazareth. And each framework is equally precious in the sight of God, as it is in the world also, when it fulfils God's purpose of healing and service and not its own purpose of mastery and domination over others.

Heaven is not an environment in which we lose ourselves as we merge into the great oneness of God. Such would be a subtle death of all identity in the body of a continuum resembling stagnation rather than life. We are, on the contrary, to realize God in our own being, and then to contribute that being to the full body of creation. This is not to be interpreted as a frantic clinging on to our private self at all costs, but rather a finding of our true self for the first time. The self that we have to lose is the ego consciousness that seeks obsessively for itself at all costs, even, if need be, to the destruction of all that is alien to it. In this world the ego is a vital part of our personality, for without its strength and resilience we would not be able to exist psychically in the coarse mundane atmosphere at all; in this respect it can be compared with the physical body that we inhabit and use while we are in this world. But as we ascend the heavenly flights, so we leave the consciousness of the ego behind, and enter into the company of those who, too, are completely themselves without strain or assertiveness, which is the character of the ego in mundane work. This ego is neither discarded nor destroyed in heaven; it is taken up into the soul, of which it is, in the first place, as outgrowth specifically fashioned for earthly conditions. And so it in fact returns to its place, or organ, of origin when it is no longer required for special service.

Heaven, like hell, is to be experienced in our present life. It is here when we are at peace within ourselves and in the company of those we love. Needless to say, such a condition is not a frequent one in any particular life, nor is its duration usually prolonged. It can, paradoxically enough, as easily show itself in situations of extreme suffering and danger as in times of prosperity and comfort. The reason is that when suffering is communally borne and the hazards encompassing everyone make the duration of any individual life an open question, the personal barriers tend to drop and people at last become open with each other. They have little more to lose except their lives, and these are best preserved in an atmosphere of mutual trust. In the silence of dark foreboding punctuated by flashes of terror a remarkable opening of the personality is apt to occur; the soul is laid bare, and God is enabled to speak through the spirit as he did to the Prodigal Son at the depth of his misery. At this point we make the amazing, though obvious, discovery that the only quality we possess is our own being, and we learn that to let it shine with integrity is the great work of our life. 'And you, like the lamp, must shed light among your fellows, so that, when they see the good you do, they may give praise to your Father in heaven' (Matthew 5:16).

This is indeed the nature of the heaven inhabited by the saints in the life beyond death, remembering in this respect that the saints are not only the great ones in the history of a religious faith but also the little ones whom we once knew in the flesh, and are now working with the others for the coming Kingdom. The traditional pictures of heaven err too much in their static representation: the chosen have finally arrived and are in a state of peaceful inanimation. People often wonder what the deceased do in the world beyond death. The question is reasonable enough because our concept of intelligence and independence shows itself in action that has an end in view. All action starts in the mind, and in the afterlife, which is a mind world, the action of the blessed departed is to pray for the souls of their less fortunate brethren in the lower purgatorial realms and in hell, and also for the distracted mortals on this side of the grave. Prayer is a two-way communication: we help our living fellows and those who are in a bad state after death, whereas the saints work in the opposite direction. The earthbound souls are thus helped from two directions; while we may not actually interfere with the free will of another person, we can at least stand beside him in his travail, no matter how responsible he may personally be for its severity, and infuse him with our love, which, of course, is a divine quality. Love is the benign influence that takes the edge off fear, resentment, prejudice and anger, whether in this world or the next. So much evil action results

97

from these four qualities when they are accorded recognition and given unlimited scope. Soon they dominate the entire consciousness of the person they afflict, and he proceeds on a course of mounting violence and disorder until the cascading intensity of the malicious attitude is interrupted. This is the work of prayer, whether for those still alive in the flesh or in an afterlife state in an earthbound situation.

In our earthly condition we are very properly limited by time and space; without this limitation we would not grow in experience and nothing would ever be done. Love acts, and action of this magnitude demands sacrifice. It is essentially on this point of sacrifice that earthly life attains its great importance: there are situations here, necessary for soul growth, that cannot be reproduced in any other milieu. It is on this account that the act of suicide is so wrong, though, of course, all tragedies may have extenuating circumstances, and the judgement is divine rather than human. When we attain the vista of the afterlife, time and space do not disappear so much as become the subject of our own altered awareness. In hell everything seems to grind to a halt as it does if we are lost in unlit caves or caught between floors in a lift before, in either instance, anyone has come to our rescue. In heaven, even on this side of life, time appears to pass by with amazing rapidity. Likewise, the space of hell is much more concentrated and dark than that of heaven, which is open, capacious and radiant. In both environments there is some aspect of time and space, though of a different order to our world-conditioned variety. The situation in dreams may shed as much light on the situation as we can comprehend at present. My own intuition has shown me that aspects of dreams may cast a light on the life ahead of us after the severance of the physical body.

The important fact seems to be that the situations of hell, heaven and the intermediate state are not totally dissimilar from the world plane. There is a psychic osmosis between the living and the dead (remembering that all are alive in God), and the blessed ones, whether in this life or the next, are active servants of the whole under the direction of God. The angelic hosts are a special group who work in collaboration with the saints in all their works. It is our spiritual obtuseness that separates us from the knowledge of the intermediate psychic world and its more spiritual horizons. The created world is one, and the more spiritually developed the person, the more in contact he is with all levels of reality. We find ourselves in the company of those with whom we feel most of home, but there can be no final segregation of any group of creatures, for we are all parts of the one body. Pascal saw truly that Christ will remain in agony until the end of the world, even though he is rightly described as presiding in eternal glory with the Father in heaven. But heaven is not an exclusive realm set aside for the saintly ones. It is, on the contrary, a boundless realm whose limits are the ability of the countless creatures to enter it.

Jesus' observation that a camel can get through a needle's eye more easily than a rich person can enter heaven explains the situation perfectly: the prerequisite for entry into heavenly life is the resolve to leave self behind. This does not include our own identity, which is precious in the sight of God, but the various accessories we have accumulated in our life on earth. None of these is necessarily bad on its own, but when it is used to complement our identity, it subtly takes over our life and becomes an idol. We become associated with the particular gift or quality we esteem, and our precious identity is obscured by it. The bulk of the gift and ourselves cannot traverse the narrow road that brings us to the heavenly gate; it cannot get through the space that is made to accommodate ourselves alone. The accessories we have acquired in life's toil are not of themselves deleterious to our spiritual progress; it is our tendency to appropriate them for ourselves that causes us to stumble. If we can guard them as stewards, and give them freely but wisely to those around us, they become a blessing for many. Then we may enter the heavenly state disembarrassed of all possessions, at the same time making that entry more available to others in our company.

In heaven we can be ourselves and enjoy the company of others who are themselves also. The concern is not primarily of moral values but of authenticity. When we are fully ourselves, the dark, acquisitive side of our nature seems to drop away, and the soul in its pristine freshness can unfold. At the same time we can allow others to be themselves also and take delight in their uniqueness. Comparisons and competition give way to co-operation and collaboration in a scheme of healing that involves every living creature. It is the power of God working through vibrant souls that initiates this social movement, whose end is the complete liberation of all living forms from the hell of isolation to the heaven of harmonious intimacy, in which each develops to his zenith for the service of the whole.

The statement, repeated on several occasions, in the first chapter of the Book of Genesis, that what God created was intrinsically good, is profoundly true. Furthermore, as the great mystics have known, God has left a witness of himself in the height of the human soul, a witness that cannot be perverted or defiled. That witness of God in the spirit of man will never consent to any action that offends the law of love, that works evil on any creature. When we reach a knowledge of the heavenly spheres this witness governs our lives, and at last we cease absolutely to do what is evil and work tirelessly for the good. This is indeed the work of those who inhabit the heavenly realm. It must not be imagined that they have finally arrived, that they are no longer involved in the sufferings of those in other dimensions of existence. They are simply in a state of continual grace in which they can serve God faithfully, the end of which service is the raising to new life of all that is downtrodden, diseased and disconsolate. As we have already noted, the human tragedy is not so much one of native evil as of mortal weakness: the spirit is willing, but the flesh is weak. In heaven there is a psychosomatic unity of accord; in this world the chosen work unanimously for the good of all under the direction of God, while in the unseen realms beyond mortal death the saints are continually about God's business. The great work is to change the hearts and minds of those who wield power, so that they may think peace to one another and act accordingly. This change of heart is not so much a manipulation of other people's lives as a bringing to their inner awareness of a dimension of reality to which they had previously been insensitive, if not completely closed.

When Christ came on earth it was to proclaim that the Kingdom of God was close to everyone on the way. To be in his presence was to taste that Kingdom, for one was accepted for what one was as the first step in becoming what one was meant to be, a child of God in the nature of Christ. Heaven can never be exclusive of anyone; it is we who exclude ourselves by our faulty list of priorities. The statement of Christ that no one can serve both God and money is especially relevant in this respect. While we pay first allegiance to the things of this world, we are imprisoned in the world together with all the possessions we have amassed. Indeed, the possessions easily assume the silent authority of warders in our self-imposed prison. Possessions separate us from our fellows: we distrust them lest they rob us, while they envy us, even attributing their own unsatisfactory lifestyles to our cupidity. And, of course, there is substance to all these attitudes of mind. The treasures of heaven, as Jesus taught, are incorruptible and cannot be appropriated selfishly by others. When our treasure is in God and our fellow man, our heart is already in heaven.

The person who knows heaven as a constant state of the soul, whether in this life or, much more probably, in the life beyond mortal death, has declared his allegiance for God. He has opted for the way of good, and his presence is a beacon of light to all those treading wearily on the long, often dispiriting path of life. To declare one's allegiance for God does not simply entitle one to dwell in the habitations of the blessed; it places on one the responsibility to get out on God's business into the world of sordid disfigurement, to spread the gospel of peace in places where war alone is known, to be prepared to give up one's life for even the least of our fellow creatures. This life is the soul identity, which is to grow in love and wisdom until time itself ends in the coming in glory of Christ in the universe. The grain of wheat remains a solitary lifeless thing unless it falls into the ground and dies, but if it dies it bears a rich harvest. This teaching of John 12:24 has to be repeated constantly even in the course of our life on earth, and in the realm of heaven death and rebirth are a constant way towards universal restitution. Though our soul identity is our most precious individual attribute, as it is sacrificed for the sake of others, so it grows in stature, taking in itself the knowledge of all whom it has encountered, thus expanding itself to include multitudes of creatures. It is in this way that the second commandment attains its quintessence: we can love our neighbour as ourself because we establish our neighbour's identity within ourself. This transaction is impossible on a strictly logical level, for we cannot be one and the other at the same time. But on a mystical level the criteria of logic are extended (rather than suspended), for now we attain a knowledge of God in whom all things coincide. In this state of extended consciousness we are more fully ourselves than ever before, and a knowledge beyond human understanding becomes available to us. St Paul writes thus of this knowledge, 'With deep roots and firm foundations, may you be strong to grasp, with all God's people, what is the breadth and length and height and depth of the love of Christ, and to know it, though it is beyond knowledge. So may you attain to fullness of being, the fullness of God himself' (Ephesians 3:18–19).

In the end the state of heaven has to include everyone, because the absence of even one creature diminishes it, and it is therefore not completely heavenly. No one in heaven can be in a state of joyous abandon with the knowledge that there are creatures in distress anywhere in the universe. The openness of the soul in heaven brings with it a sensitivity to all the world's pain, and with that awareness comes an ineradicable desire to relieve it. It is indeed true that the souls of the virtuous are at peace with God, but their work is to bring the knowledge of that spiritual peace down to the turmoil of the outside world. To leave heavenly peace is a great sacrifice, but its motive is pure love: to bring that peace to whomsoever will receive it at the present moment in time. There is no greater work than this, for it prepares the way for Christ's second coming.

11

The Cosmic Conflict:
The Claims of Darkness and Light

There are two dominant powers in our world; of the greater universe we can speak only in analogy, but inasmuch as the spiritual consciousness embraces all worlds in the one divine reality, we may be reasonably sure that the conditions of our world are a part of the greater whole and not in any way dissimilar from it. The dominant powers are those of good and evil, or light and darkness in the language of the Fourth Gospel and the first letter of St John. This dualism is not a primary fact of life, for God is the sole Creator of all things, and in him there is light without any darkness at all (1 John 1:5). All that God has made is fundamentally good, but it has to experience its own being and actualize itself. This is the law of growth that is an immediate corollary of the life of the creature. Thus, the infant may be perfectly fashioned, but it establishes its perfection only as it grows to adulthood, and is able to control its own inner functions to the extent of a glowing maturity. As we read in Hebrews 5:7–10, Christ himself, son as he was, learned obedience in the school of suffering, and once perfected became the source of eternal salvation for all who obey him, named by God high priest in the succession of Melchizedek. This perfection was attained in living the life of a common man among the multitude, and offering up prayers and petitions, in great suffering, to God who was able to deliver him from the grave. It was his humble submission that enabled his prayer to be heard. In this way Jesus moved unobtrusively towards the supreme darkness of crucifixion, thus assuming the darkness of the world, and then by virtue of his spiritual excellence was found worthy of a supreme resurrection in the light of God's presence.

Another person, however, even as gifted as Jesus himself, might have spurned the divine guidance and moved defiantly in his own way towards domination and the subjugation of all his fellows so that they became mere slaves of his purpose. This was indeed Jesus' third temptation by the devil in the wilderness, according to St Matthew's account. Had he succumbed to the wiles of the evil one, he could have attained world dominion, but the one in final charge would have been the devil, and he rather than Jesus would have exerted the definitive influence on the cosmos. Whenever we succumb to the power of matter, the evil one triumphs, and darkness overcomes light. Whenever we choose the way of God, we enter into light, and the way to resurrection is shown us. But the journey is arduous, even heartbreaking, as the lives of many of the prophets have indicated. It too has to enter into the darkness as a prelude to a universal resurrection into the light.

All this consideration posits a conscious, intelligent force of darkness, an overpowering presence of evil in the universe, a presence of personal identity no less real in essence than the personal presence of God. If the personal God of monotheism loves all that is created, so the personal evil one, the devil, is equally aware of the creation, but desires it for personal gain so that he may eventually be the master of the universe. Let it be said at once that the genesis of evil is a result of the primary creative act of God, by whom all things are made. God may not have willed the emergence of evil, but he could not avoid it when he bestowed free will on his rational creatures, whether human or angelic. To use that divine gift of free choice on a personal, acquisitive basis is much more immediately attractive than offering it in humble dedication to God and one's fellow creatures. The vision of world dominion is far more compelling than one of service for the good of the created whole. The end of this fateful choice is seen when we survey the course of selfish action as directed by the evil one, traditionally depicted as a fallen angel of immense resource and malice.

The way of the evil one is to offer us all manner of good things, so that our material wants are satisfied, our diseases healed and our personal magnetism is enhanced. Soon we are subtly changed as individuals: revelling in our own personal power and material possessions we start to glorify the one who effected this magnificent transformation in our condition. This is in fact precisely the recompense exacted by the power of evil, that everyone should bow down to his person and worship him. In so doing the identity of the creature is quietly diminished, as his will is progressively usurped by the all-embracing power that infiltrates his personality; eventually the person is swallowed up in a mass obedience to the supreme power. The integrity of the creature is undermined; the person is seduced into a surrender of his God-inspired purity of judgement and intent. His spiritual aspiration falters and his ideals are brought down to the level of general corruption that typifies a people of heedless activity and spiritual blindness. Eventually he ceases to respond to the insistent call of the Holy Spirit to assume the full nature of a son of God, instead retreating into the dungheap of vice and delinquency.

This is the way of the devil, whose nature is that of the antiChrist, when he gains ascendancy over his deluded victims; he subtly clouds their soul consciousness so that they are deflected from acting in a morally responsible fashion. Instead they behave like a herd of cattle, comparable to the Gadarene swine in which the evil spirits exorcized by Jesus took refuge; the end of the pigs was destruction in the nearby lake, a type of end in store for the possessed humans also. There is a mysterious and highly significant passage in the Gospel where Christ instructs his disciples not to be afraid of those who have the power to destroy the body, but fear in no uncertain fashion those who have the power to destroy both soul and body in hell (Matthew 10:28). On one level of reality the soul is immortal, inasmuch as it is God's creation and God loves every created thing. But the power of evil can so dominate a person that his soul consciousness is totally obliterated; he discards his human identity and behaves irrationally, like a coarse animal in a large herd, entirely under the direction of the evil one.

This terrible sequence is seen in the course of mob violence. The precious power of discrimination, the fruit of our individual integrity and the very spark of our identity, is blurred and occluded. Devoid of this light of responsibility, the individual is tumultuously overriden by the emotional surge of the crowd and is rendered capable of committing the grossest acts of destructive cruelty, acts that the same person in a state of calm and prayerful awareness would reject in abhorrence. From all this we can see how the antiChrist acts: first the awareness of the person is dulled and duped into a torpid complacency as the confidence is won by acts of supply and apparent generosity. The freedom of the will is then unobtrusively abdicated, so that the victim leans ever more in dependence and trust on the source that has come to his assistance. The evil one battens on the soul consciousness of his victim, whence issues the free will with its capacity to choose and make decisions. In this way the torpid, unguarded awareness lets in evil destructive powers that rob the person of his freedom. As the soul is taken over and the personal freedom of action is set on one side, so the individual becomes inextricably enslaved to the devil, who proceeds to attack and dismember the soul until it becomes a pulp of discrete personal data that are dissipated into the general psychic milieu of the afterlife.

We see this horrifying trend of events whenever a secular agency takes absolute control and organizes a composite group of people around it. Despotic political regimes are one obvious example, but so has been the Church throughout the ages. In this respect the concept of the Church embraces all religious traditions; their aim is to bring the people to the ultimate reality that is called God when a personal, loving dimension is envisaged as the result of an encounter with the divine in nature, or with the numinous as transmitted psychically in art or in deep personal relationships. The summation in the main Christian stream is the sacrament of the Eucharist, which in turn finds its peak in the hush of silence that descends in the moment of sudden cosmic awareness at the time of receiving the elements and thanking God for them afterwards. It is, indeed, the silence that brings the Deity in close relationship with us, whereas the preceding liturgy, splendid as it may be, serves rather to put us in the right frame of mind to receive the divine guest who is also our eternal host.

When a Church takes this function of divine encounter and human development to full sonship with God for granted, it is in great jeopardy of becoming enmeshed in a web of power politics, whether intrinsic to its structure, related to the country in which it functions, or as part of the world scene. While none of this is primarily wrong – indeed, it is an inevitable part of every individual's work to become involved in such matters, especially if the person is intelligent and compassionate – it can soon manifest demonic overtones as the institution or a particular variety of political and economic involvement holds sway. It is in our ceaseless aspiration to the Deity, the one alone who transcends institutions and political theories while infusing them all with love according to the ability of their servants to receive that love, that salvation lies. Jesus put this even more starkly when he said, 'Set your mind on God's kingdom and his justice before everything else, and all the rest will come to you as well' (Matthew 6:33). The converse is equally true: if any thought other than the love of God and his law of service in the world guides us in our ambitions, the result will be enslavement to the evil powers. We often forget that the choice set before us is one of life and spiritual death, of light and darkness. If we choose the way of light and life, we will certainly be tested in the fire of experience and tempted to self-gratification on the one hand and despair on the other – Jesus himself was spared neither temptation and to excess. But we shall not be overcome; this teaching, enunciated by St Paul in Romans 8 in a most splendid outburst and more tenderly by Julian of Norwich in her *Revelations of Divine Love*, is the essence of the spiritual hope. It is certainly seldom fulfilled even tentatively in such short earthly life, and indeed the sufferings of innumerable people on the altar of incurable disease, man's constant inhumanity to man, and the various natural disasters that rock the world seem to point to the delusion if not the actual lie enshrined in such a world view. But the test is always the same: could we possibly want to return to our state before we saw the light that drew us on? A few have actively retreated in this way, but all that has been left for them is emptiness, cynicism and a dreary negativity that refuses to see value in anything outside the data of the physical senses, whose temporal duration is limited enough even in the life of one body. The question – and the answer – is always that of Peter when he is asked whether he, too, like so many others in the Master's entourage, would prefer to leave him now, 'Lord, to whom shall we go? Your words are words of eternal life' (John 6:68). The cosmic conflict reveals the eternal nature of Christ, now no longer manifested by admirable soul-qualities, but a living, transforming presence in the world.

If, on the other hand, we choose the way of darkness and death, which means in effect selecting a path that magnifies our own interests to the expense of all other people, we shun the promptings of our own soul which we, as it were, lease to the convenience of those who are even more unscrupulous than we are. This somewhat dramatic presentation of a life situation occurs when we choose the lesser way for our own convenience. The type of person who hounds a fellow creature because of his racial or religious background or because of his unusual lifestyle is one who has chosen the domain of darkness for the kingdom of light. By identifying himself with persecutors, who are invariably the tools of the evil one inasmuch as their soul consciousness is completely taken over by forces of hatred and destruction, he surrenders something of his God-given identity to them, who in turn surrender everything to the dark forces that govern so much material life.

How, then, can we distinguish between the powers of light and darkness in our present climactic world situation – it is climactic on account of the enormous scientific and technical advancements escalating year by year together with the greater sophistication of the younger generation devoid, in turn, of any great reverence for the unseen dimension of reality? The powers of darkness have, as we have already observed, the capacity to assume a bright glitter that can deceive the unwary if not the very elect. This statement could be transposed to the devil quoting Scripture in Jesus' three temptations; the word of God itself is not self-interpreting.

We are the interpreters according to what God has shown us of himself in our private lives, our natural common sense, and the tradition of which we are a part. Although in a period of great anxiety we may have to act completely alone, we are not alone if we can pray, for then we are united to God, and the mighty communion of saints are with us also. Here we see the juxtaposition of humility and responsibility: once aligned to the heavenly hosts we are strengthened to do the work that must be done, and we, like Jesus, are both servant and master. We can distinguish a power of darkness by the hatred it exudes; it works towards the destruction that stands in its path to dominion, first local, then regional and finally of the whole world. It cannot learn, save how to be more effective in its actions, but of the nature and aspirations of any opposed to its advance it is insensitive if not culpably ignorant. In the end its supporters are levelled down to a common mould, one that is most useful to its infamous ends.

By contrast, love emanates from a power of light. This is something of a different order from warmth or even affection, which I am prepared to imagine an evil influence can also present to the unwary. Love acts by giving up itself, even to death if need be, for the sake of its friend, who in the final analysis is everyone around us, the neighbour in the Parable of the Good Samaritan. This in turn necessitates a love of oneself so complete that one no longer feels threatened by anyone else, let alone has any desire to abuse, denigrate or destroy him. In the face of that love, which is for everyone if it is real – for love, unlike affection, has no favourites – the beloved is shown the light, and unless he is stony-hearted and recalcitrant, he will move of his own free will to that light. 'The people who walked in darkness have seen a great light: light has dawned upon them, dwellers in a land as dark as death. . . . For a boy has been born for us, a son given to us to bear the symbol of dominion on his shoulder; and he shall be called in purpose wonderful, in battle God-like, Father for all time, Prince of peace' (Isaiah 9:2, 6). To be a follower of the Messiah is to be filled with new life so that every faculty is renewed and the whole personality illuminated and transfigured. The identity sparkles in triumphant affirmation, but it does not revel in individualistic gestures.

109

It rather adds its own contribution to the mighty fellowship of saints, the ones alive on earth being in psychic osmosis with those beyond death. By serving in the body of the Most High each organ, or member, attains the apogee of its own unique excellence.

In the mighty conflict of spiritual values – a better term than mere moral ones, for morality can be used to justify many hard, unloving attitudes to ways of life that are unsatisfactory but need understanding and love rather than unremitting judgement – our adversaries, as we have already noted, are in the intermediary psychic realm. In the Letter to the Ephesians, certainly Pauline in inspiration if not wholly written by St Paul himself, the adversaries are clearly stated to be cosmic powers, the authorities and potentates of this dark world and the superhuman forces of evil in the heavens (Ephesians 6:12). It is indeed in the suprahuman dimension that the origin of evil is to be located, but it finds an easy entry in the hearts (or souls) of all those who are unwary, sluggish in the life of prayer and sacrament, and whose private lives are thoughtless and selfish. The social realist might wonder at the sequence of personal defects I have described: surely the way of private life is the most important of the three? But a life devoted to social service and praiseworthy political action soon becomes infiltrated with the forces of evil if it is not well guarded by constant awareness and a primary dedication to God. We are never so dangerous as when fighting on the side of righteousness with weapons tarnished with hatred. The history of various revolutionary movements, especially those of our own century, underlines the power of evil to corrupt admirable idealism when the protagonist is convinced that he alone is right, and all others are wrong. Furthermore, if a person is wrong in the estimation of such a biased partisan, it follows that he is evil, a henchman of the devil. And so prosecutions and terror follow, all in the name of an admirable political and economic theory, which in the end fails to bring any other result than slavery in a new disguise. The reason for this sequence is the exclusion of love, which comes from God. So in the end the power of darkness has won a mighty victory. If the emanation of evil is hatred, its end is enslavement. Just as in the prisons of old each inmate was given a special number and recognized by that number rather than by his own name, so the powers of darkness render their victims faceless, nameless and apparently soulless. The process is a descent into hell, in a way a hell more terrible than the sphere of isolation reserved, as it were, for the erring individual who has failed to repent of his selfish, destructive way of life. This individual is still in contact with his soul identity, even if he cannot place it adequately in relation to his altered situation. The masses led by the power of evil into acts of unspeakably vile cruelty have surrendered their unique being and are now a nameless, faceless mass of screaming animals. In the end it is certain that a return to sanity will take place, preferably in this life or else in the life after death, and then comes a prolonged period of remorse for actions that cannot be altered. It should be recognized that the state of hell is irreversible by human action. The statement, 'And as it is the lot of men to die once, and after death comes judgement, so Christ was offered once to bear the burden of men's sins, and will appear a second time, sin done away, to bring salvation to those who are watching for him' (Hebrews 9:27–28), indicates that deliverance from hell is due to divine mercy, but we have always to be ready to receive Christ, the ultimate person of redemption of creation from the prison of everlasting, but not eternal, hell.

The passage in the Letter to the Ephesians already quoted, advises us to use truth, integrity, the gospel of peace, faith, salvation, and finally the power of the Holy Spirit who will give us the right words when the occasion requires them. The need for unceasing prayer is emphasized. Truth is not easy to know until we are at peace within, where lies our integrity and our hidden treasure. Peace in this context is a state of inner oneness with God, a state in which we can listen to various different points of view, and without having our own integrity threatened, can learn from many different types of people and sources of information. A particularly beguiling aspect of hell, or rather a niche in the general hellish atmosphere, is one frequented by those who know they are right, especially in matters of global significance in the realms of politics and economics. They look down in pity on those who cannot agree with them. But many such dogmatists have never experienced the circumstances against which they now so fervently campaign. In many current problems of this type the consensus veers clearly, and often for very good reason, in a particular direction. It is nevertheless better to try to effect a reconciliation or a more considered, gradual approach to an intractable problem than to precipitate such discontent that serious disturbances break out which cause widespread suffering. In the course of this unattractive suffering the noisy protagonists from afar usually beat a measured retreat.

The faith that serves in the cosmic conflict is provided by the cloud of witnesses that are eternally around us leading us inexorably in the direction of Christ, 'on whom faith depends from start to finish: Jesus who, for the sake of the joy that lay ahead of him, endured the cross, making light of its disgrace, and has taken his seat at the right hand of the throne of God' (Hebrew 12:2). What he stood for and vindicated is a new understanding of reality, that renewal and total spiritualization are the apex of the creative process which continues as long as time remains. Salvation comes from his action in every life provided we have the humility and trust to introduce him to every facet of our existence, every part of our inner life, for God's courtesy is such that he does not intrude into our private lives or invite himself unexpectedly. But tragedy can strike without warning, and then God's presence is eagerly welcomed. Indeed, it seems to be a rule, almost a law of nature, that we do not seek God until we are brought very low, so low that we can see clearly in front of us with vision unobstructed by any fantasies or illusions. Perhaps it is better so, for then at least we can value God's presence instead of taking it for granted as Adam and Eve did before the Fall. God created us in order that we should fulfil our own destiny, even to become his sons in fact as well as by creation. It is more important for us to be true to our nature than any other consideration, even the worship of God. But until we attain right worship of God, we will never know the riches that lie untapped within us, and we will be in constant danger of being seduced and corrupted by the dark forces of the universe which already have their representatives in the human psyche.

Balance is the centre of all progressive motion. It is the subtle interplay of light and shade, of warmth and cold, of youth and age, that are the bases of enduring relationships, or as Jacob Boehme put it, 'In yes and no all things subsist' (*Of the Supersensual Life*, Dialogue 1). Much traditional propriety was orderly, well-mannered, cold and very boring; the same applies to even the most excellent religion when it becomes self-assured, triumphalistic and socially stratified. The surface is plausible enough, but the depths are uncharted. By contrast the permissive society is disorderly and frequently ill-mannered, but its individual members are often acutely concerned about social and political justice in a way that only a few eccentric people would have been in time gone by. The irresponsibility shown in some personal relationships is balanced by a depth of concern for the underdog who was often ignored in the past. Neither the old nor the new is adequate on its own; the old is dead, the new is constantly dying, but from the ashes of its concern and the order of the past a new way could be opened by the power of God in whom alone there is a coincidence of all opposites.

This is indeed the essence of the new dispensation: a flowing together of previously opposing forces, each set on its way as the only measure of perfection. The spiritual battle was the symbol of the past: the righteous won and the wicked were defeated, either suffering death or at least severe punishment. Repentance alone secured some mitigation of sentence. The denouement of modern military conflict has shown the inadequacy, almost the fallacy, of this approach. In the end there is no peace and certainly no permanent victors. Those that are the losers plot subterranean vengeance, while the victors exploit their conquest to the detriment of the other parties. The same scheme applies to less dramatic conflicts in a social or even a family milieu. Above all, no one grows in spiritual stature, for each is concerned only about himself, his rights, and his reputation. When we have learned to hold fast to God, however we conceive him, we shall have transcended this petty, destructive domain of individual satisfaction and death, and moved to something of the new life in Christ.

Then the wolf shall live with the sheep,
    and the leopard lie down with the kid;
    the calf and the young lion shall grow up together,
    and a little child shall lead them;
    the cow and the bear shall be friends,
    and their young shall lie down together.
The lion shall eat straw like cattle;
    the infant shall play over the hole of the cobra,
    and the young child dance over the viper's nest.
They shall not hurt or destroy in all my holy mountain;
    for as the waters fill the sea,
    so shall the land be filled with the knowledge of the Lord.
                      (Isaiah 11:6–9)

12

The Coming Again

When the cosmic conflict is at its height, the forces of darkness set on universal destruction evenly balanced by the forces of light intent on a victory for their cause, there will come a moment of dark, poignant silence. The minds of all rational creatures will be focused on a point of absolute awareness which will contain nothing. Out of the dark silence there will come a luminous glow that will be intensified rapidly until it becomes a light so radiant that its rays will transfigure all the world. The Lord will come to claim his own, who are all created things, but now they will be utterly transfigured. Death and decay will have been transcended by a new creation in which the whole living universe will be lifted up to God himself. Heaven and earth will have passed completely away, but the Word of Life will have created all things new.

The creation story started in the darkness of utter material emptiness, though the Spirit of God in fact fills all things. In the end the cosmos itself will be lifted out of the sequence of mortality to enter upon the liberty and splendour of the children of God. And then all will meet on the summit of the mountain of transfiguration, each bringing their own kind with them in their own heaven. As they reach the top, men of all races and religions will establish their common unity as they have penetrated their own tradition to its heart and attained its summit. They will find that they now speak with one language and know one Christ who is the destination of all the great religions, to whose coming again they had all looked forward according to their own particular tradition and whom they now see in the faces of all those around them. As St John puts it, 'Here and now, dear friends, we are God's children; what we shall be has not yet been disclosed, but we know that when it is disclosed we shall be like him, because we shall see him as he is' (1 John 3:2).

When this happens, the great second advent leading to the final appearing of the Lord, time will have been lifted up into eternity. The advent could be very soon, but in fact time is only a symbol of our present incompleteness. When we are ready he will appear as a supreme cosmic event. He will also change the hearts of all from stone to flesh, the flesh of the spiritual body. None will be excluded. It is the work of all those who consider themselves servants of the Most High to labour day and night for the conversion of all men to God, not as a theological abstraction but as a living, driving force that resurrects all life from personal illusion to universal participation. 'Then the Lord shall become king over all the earth; on that day the Lord shall be one Lord and his name the one name' (Zechariah 14:9). Meanwhile, let us keep awake for the great arrival.